DeBAITed Deaths Unknown Face

All rights are reserved. No part of this book may be reproduced in any manner whatsoever, including Internet usage, without the permission from the publisher by a notarized contract of parties, except by review. This novel is a work of fiction. Any references of historical events, real people, and/or real locations are used fictitiously. Any names, characters, places and/or incidents are the product of the imagination. Any resemblances to the actual events, locations, incidents, or characters living or dead, are entirely coincidental.

ISBN 978-0-615-74407-0
Copyright © 2011
By Kolendra Jackson

ACKNOWLEDGEMENTS

First, I must give honor to God as He is the head of my life and Jesus is Lord of my salvation. I am truly thankful for this gift of writing and the ability to use this gift to be an inspiration and blessing to others. I give God the glory for my passion to reach people on all levels.

Mom & Dad thank you for all of your support. Rashad, my brother, I appreciate your significance as a role model for my children. To my children Josalyn & Josh – all I do is for you.

To my editor and dear friend Regina Anderson of Visionary Writing Services, I can't thank you enough for all of the hours that you have poured into my life.

Finally, I would like to reflect on the memory of my Grandma Rosa who has passed since the initial release. I am indebted for her unconditional love. The first prayer I learned was Psalm 23 which she taught me in my youth during troublesome times. She explained the meaning of Jesus' promises and emphasized His love for me. I'll never depart from it. I am very grateful for every moment we shared. Rest in Peace.

DeBAITed Deaths Unknown Face

INTRODUCTION

This novel is dedicated to every woman who has had to fight for anything as a wife, mother, sister, friend, and mistress. It is for every man who has never really understood the extent of a woman's love. This novel is graphic, it is bold, it is heartfelt, and it is real-fiction.

Everyone has a past. Everyone has a secret. Everyone has a price. The unexpected deaths of loved ones are at times the fault of our spirits. The face of death is often times the face of those who are the closest to us, visible, yet unknown.

Divine intervention passes over all of us and it is during that season we must acknowledge the danger that surrounds us and surrender to the spirit that lives within us.

Grace and mercy are gifts and it is the power of prayer which actually changes things. However, prayer is not magic. It doesn't make things happen instantly. Often times we are in the midst of turmoil, heartache, grief, and need before we even consider praying. Prayer should never be the last resort.

Good and/or bad we reap the harvest of the seeds that we have sown. Bait can be disguised as love and loyalty, but fear, greed, and selfishness will always have its' own perfectly masked agenda.

"DeBAITed Deaths Unknown Face."

DeBAITed Deaths Unknown Face

BACK IN THE DAY

Monique, six months pregnant, sat frustrated in a crowded lobby waiting for her admissions counselor at the University of Georgia. Devastated by her decision to drop out of college, she envied all the other young ladies and how they seemed to be excited and carefree; only worrying about themselves and not the burden of an unborn child. She rubbed her belly as she wondered how to break the news to her boyfriend Rick that her baby was not *his*. The stress of hurting Rick broke Monique's heart. She knew Rick would hate her, but worst of all she knew that the affair which resulted in her pregnancy would end Rick's friendship with his best friend Mike.

Her sexual affair with Mike had been exotic, and Monique's mind frequently visited their late nights. She often lusted after the 6'2, strong, athletic, dark chocolate delight. Her body yearned for him as she frequently envisioned him touching her. *'Stop it!'* She thought, as she dismissed her memories.

"Monique Blake?" the counselor called.

"Yes, that's me," Mo replied as she walked towards the admissions counselor with her withdrawal form.

After her day at the campus, Monique called her sister Naja, hoping they could meet for dinner. When her sister didn't answer, Monique left her a voicemail.

> "Hey, Sis. I really need some advice. I've really messed up and I am scared that Rick is going to snap. Call me. I want us to meet for dinner before they come over tonight. Love you to pieces."

Instead of Naja returning the call she listened to the voicemail and sent Monique a text message that read: *"I've already planned private evening arrangements."*

Naja had no regard for anyone else unless they were of a benefit to her. She hated Monique and *her* family.

DeBAITed Deaths Unknown Face

Her emotional hatred kept her from feeling close to her sister and the African American family who raised her. Naja wanted her own family.

Her plans that evening were important and the simple worries of Monique irritated her. She dreaded Monique's telephone calls, especially when she called to talk about Rick. As she tried to ignore the vibrations from her cell phone, she applied makeup over her freckles. After back to back phone calls, it became apparent that Monique was not going to give up. After ignoring the first six calls, she finally decided to answer. She owned a cold, intimidating voice. "What is it already? I don't have much time Mo."

Monique felt the heaviness of her own heart. She wanted Naja to sympathize with her and listen to her reasons of why she couldn't keep lying to Rick, but Naja simply did not care.

Naja shrugged her shoulders and stated, "Rick's ass needs to walk. You don't need him or anybody else. You have to quit depending on me and Monte to bail you out."

"Monte? Who said anything about him and what does my brother have to do with this?" Mo asked.

Naja resented Monique's relationship with Monte. As siblings, they were all raised to love each other, but Monte always favored his biological sister, Monique, over his adopted sister Naja. Besides, Naja grew closer to the other outsider, their half-brother Orlando, born as a result of an extramarital affair.

"You didn't have to say anything. I already know you. You want me to tell you that it was okay for you to screw around, get knocked up and lie about it. Frankly, I couldn't care less, but I also know that if I don't help you, you're going to whine to Monte like a little brat and he is just as much to blame as you. Rick and Mike are his friends Mo. What in the hell were you thinking?"

"That doesn't have anything to do with it. Monte is

DeBAITed Deaths Unknown Face

'my' brother. He will always be there, period. It does not matter who his friends are or who I choose to sleep with. You keep Monte out of this. I called to share my feelings with you, not to be judged. Besides, I don't have to ask Monte to bail me out. He would never stand by and watch either of them mistreat me, no matter what."

Naja held the line on mute while she snorted a line of cocaine and slipped into her lingerie.

After a long silence, Monique spoke up, "Why do you disapprove of my relationship with Rick? What has he ever done to you?"

Naja hated being challenged. "You should be glad that isn't Rick's child. Rick is dangerous, but you are just too naïve to see it. Hell, I think it's best for you to be pregnant by your own kind."

Monique knew how selfish Naja could be. She knew Naja resented the world because of her own personal circumstances of being a white woman adopted by an African American family.

"See Naja, I knew it would be a matter of time before you played the race card. You make Rick being white a problem because you're white. Just because your parents weren't shit doesn't mean Rick is the same way. And what do you mean 'my kind'? We are the same kind of people who took you in. What difference does it make if Rick is white? What is your problem?" Monique pleaded.

"Mo I have to go. I have plans of my own and if everything goes right with this new client tonight, I won't be around to save your ass. I have bigger fish to fry so it would be nice for you to get it together and repay me a few favors. It is still all about the Benjamin's," Naja replied as she smiled at herself in the mirror.

DeBAITed Deaths Unknown Face

"Well, it will all end tonight. I called Monte and asked him to meet at my place. I hope he gets there before Rick does tonight. When Mike arrives, then I'll break the news," Monique sighed. "I am scared out of my mind, but at least Monte will be here to protect me."

Naja chuckled. "Good ole Monte boy is always saving your ass. Call me if you're still alive afterwards."

"I'll be fine. We'll talk later." Mo replied.

Naja hung up.

That evening Rick called Monique.

"Hello," Mo greeted.

"Hey, what's going on?"

"Rick, we need to talk. Can you come over?"

"Bet," Rick replied ending the call.

Rick stood 5'8 with a thin solid build. His sexy charisma complimented his low crew cut and natural clear blue eyes. He arrived a few minutes before Mike. Nervously, Monique opened the door without greeting him with a hug. At that moment he knew that his suspicions were true.

Monique wore a long sundress that complimented her small pregnant belly to symbolize a shield of protection against any violence once Rick heard her confession. She glowed like most expecting mothers, but Rick could tell that she was scared half to death.

"Are you by yourself?" Monique asked Rick as she allowed him to walk past her into the kitchen.

Rick's voice was deep and raspy. "You know Monte's out there," he replied as he scanned the refrigerator for his beer.

"I threw that beer out when I cleaned the refrigerator. Once the baby gets here, I'm not going to be with all that drinking and partying anymore Rick. And how am I supposed to know Monte is with you? Why didn't he get out?"

He looked at her. His eyes changed from blue to green, an indication that his mood was changing for the worst.

DeBAITed Deaths Unknown Face

"You play to many games Mo. You always call Monte for back up in your bullshit. What do you have to tell me? Just say it."

Mo knew that she couldn't string Rick along much longer before he snapped so she stalled by going into the restroom until Mike arrived. As she washed her hands, she heard a knock on the door.

"Oh Lawd," she sighed on the verge of tears. "Hold on," she yelled.

By the time Mo got to her front door, Rick was already welcoming Mike into her home. They were slapping hands and exchanging greetings the way guys do. Mike was cool and collected as he braced himself for the news. Before anyone began to speak, Monte walked into the apartment and took a seat at the bar next to Rick. Mike sat on the edge of the couch and Monique stood in the center of the floor facing all the men in the room.

Her words were shaky and her voice trembled but the outspoken Monique let her words practically fall out of her mouth,

"Look Rick, I have been messing with Mike and the baby isn't *yours*."

Tears flooded her face as she felt the tension in the room lock her eardrums. Not surprised, the friends didn't respond. Mo spoke again.

"I lied to you Rick. I had a period after we had sex and then I had sex with Mike. It was unprotected and this baby is his."

DeBAITed Deaths Unknown Face

She had finally come clean, and the room was silent. Rick sat back against the back of the barstool in a state of shock. He had always felt that someone else was the father but he couldn't fathom how she could do this... with *Mike*. They were like brothers. For as long as Rick could remember their friendship had been solid. Mike was relieved. He was proud to gain confirmation and yet still a part of him was uncomfortable. He knew that his childhood friend was mentally unstable.

Rick and Mike met in foster care after Mike's old man had killed his mother and Rick's mother had died of cancer. As a child, Rick had also suffered years of sexual and physical abuse. The boys had become friends all those years ago.

Rick couldn't move. *"Damn!"* he thought.

Mike stood prepared to defend himself. He and Monte both kept their eyes on Rick, but Rick didn't move. He was hurt. His body sizzled with anger as his complexion turned beet red. His head hung low but his eyes were glued on Monique's belly. Instantly, he resented the innocent child that she carried. He never once looked over at Mike, but mentally he vowed to make him pay this debt of their friendship in full. Rick stood and walked past Monique as he left without saying a word to anyone. Monte grabbed his sister as she sobbed into his shoulder. Mike took his seat on the couch. At that moment, he knew that he would have to watch his back for the rest of his life. Rick was dangerous only because of circumstance. He had violent tendencies and he always seemed to be a ticking time bomb.

As different as the three men seemed, they all had one thing in common. Rick, Mike and Monte all worked for one dangerous, powerful, well connected man, David Carter.

Once Monique was alone she called Naja,
"Yes?" Naja answered.
"Well, the cat is out of the bag and no dead bodies."

DeBAITed Deaths Unknown Face

"Yea, okay. Hey it was good of you to call. I am leaving town. I have an opportunity elsewhere so I won't be around for a while."

"Are you okay? Is there anything I need to know about?" Monique asked, knowing Naja would not elaborate.

"No, I will be in touch. Just watch yourself," Naja replied, as she peeked at her evening companion between the sheets.

"What about the baby? Will you be around when it's time?"

"Not now Mo. I need to wrap my client up. Keep your panties on. We will talk soon enough."

"Smooches." Monique ended the call.

The sisters called each other weekly on Sundays during Naja's absence. Over time the communication ended.

A few months later Monique gave birth to Alex, her son with Mike. The parents never solidified a relationship but they remained platonic friends and worked as a team to provide for their son. Soon after Alex was born, Mo was finally on her feet with a stable career. Silly enough, she and Rick began another explosive affair.

That fall, before her storm, Monique was pregnant again, this time with Rick's child. Rick and Monique were in love again, yet she feared him most nights. In spite of his abuse, she believed Rick when he told her things would be different if they got married. He had even opened his heart to love Alex. When they married, things seemed better for a while. A few months of Naja's absence turned into years and although Mo cared, her sister never really gave it any thought. Mo often regretted not listening to Naja's advice. The love she felt for Rick was unhealthy. He had proven himself to be dangerous and physically abusive. She tolerated his volatile mood swings until they finally divorced.

DeBAITed Deaths Unknown Face

After a while, it seemed as if her life was changing for the better, or so she thought. Naja returned without notice. Surprisingly, she warmed up to Alex and welcomed Mo's new pregnancy, although she continued to resent Monique's role in Rick's life.

Naja had also changed drastically. She now had a multi-millionaire client named David Carter, the same David who Rick, Monte, and Mike worked for many years before. Rick was David's hit man. Now Naja wanted him, she needed him personally. While she was away, Naja gained David's trust and the opportunity to become his criminal defense lawyer. After pulling him out of a few sticky situations, she also gained his respect, but that wasn't enough for her. She desired a relationship with David. Her plan was to gain all that he was worth. She also hated his fiancée, Brenda, and vowed to cause her to crumble. Her hatred had become all consuming. She would methodically place everyone at her beck and call. She enforced her new mission to become Mrs. Carter, the widow.

DeBAITed Deaths Unknown Face

MONIQUE: Current Day

The rainy Saturday morning caused the children's softball game to be canceled, so Monique and her boys started preparing for breakfast.

"Make a choice. Do you want oatmeal with bacon or sausage with grits?" Mo asked Alex, now age nine, and Ashton age six.

"I only want sausage," Alex said.

"I only want oatmeal," Ashton said.

"Okay, okay. How about we all have pancakes with sausage instead?" offered Monique.

"Yay!" Both boys screamed in unison. "Pancakes are our favorite!"

The telephone rang as Mo stirred the batter. "Grab the phone Alex," she instructed.

"Hello? Good. We are going to eat pancakes when our mommy gets done cooking."

"Who is on the phone Alex?" Mo asked as she poured batter into the pan.

"Rick," he replied.

Before Monique could wipe her hands, Ashton began running for the phone. He took the receiver from his brother's hand and squealed into the phone. "Daddy, my tooth came out when I was eating at McDonalds and the tooth fairy left me a five dollar bill."

Rick was excited for his son. "Alright man! That's good. Save your money so you can buy yourself something cool okay."

"Okay daddy, I love you."

"I love you too Ash. Can you give your mama the phone?"

"Yes daddy, hold on."

DeBAITed Deaths Unknown Face

Still in a good mood, Mo's voice was pleasant as she took the phone from Ashton and kissed his forehead. "Go watch television in your room," she instructed. "I will call you both when breakfast is ready."

"Yes ma'am," her boys replied as they left the kitchen.

"Hello," Monique greeted as she held the phone with her shoulder so that she could continue preparing breakfast.

"What's happening?" Rick asked.

"I was just making breakfast for the boys and then we are probably just going to chill the rest of the day since it's raining so hard outside," Mo replied as she flipped another pancake.

"I wanted to come by and scoop Ash up and kick it with him for a little bit. Is that cool with you?" Rick asked.

"That will be fine, but Naja normally picks them up early on Sunday so you gotta make sure you drop him off tonight."

"Okay," Rick replied before hanging up the phone.

Rick lived in a rural area about twenty minutes south of Atlanta. He showed up around ten minutes after noon, casually dressed wearing a t-shirt, jeans, sneakers-no laces. His girlfriend, Jasmine, sat in the car. He hadn't planned for her to tag along, but when she overheard his conversation with his son, she persuaded Rick to allow her to spend the evening with him. He felt pressured as he anticipated Monique having a serious attitude as she always did with his women. Rick knocked on the door as he looked back at the car to see if Jasmine was snooping through his armrest.

"Daddy!" Ashton squealed as he opened the door.

"Hey man," Rick replied. He scooped his son up off his feet and tossed him into the air.

"Hey Rick," Alex spoke as he stepped out onto the porch with his brother.

"What's going on Alex man? How have you been doing?"

DeBAITed Deaths Unknown Face

He greeted as he placed Ashton onto his feet. He looked Alex in his dark brown eyes. For a moment Rick thought of Mike who had died in an accident witnessed by Rick, or so that is what people assumed. Nevertheless, Rick had love for Alex.

"Have you been hanging in there?"

"Yes sir, I'm good."

"We are going to hang for a while, probably catch a movie. Do you want to go?" Rick invited. Mo interrupted before Alex could answer the lingering question.

"Hey Rick, I see you made it."

"Hey Mo, wassup? Can I get a hug?" Rick flirted.

She always ignored Rick's advances. She knew he was joking. Any sign of weakness on her part would send things to a whole other level. As she handed Rick his son's backpack, she noticed Alex looking pitiful.

"What's wrong with you?" She asked Alex.

"Can I go Mommy?"

"I invited Alex too if it's okay with you," Rick added.

"What time will y'all be back?"

"No later than nine o'clock."

"Do you want to go baby?"

"Yes ma'am," Alex beamed.

She smiled too. "Okay, you can go. Thanks Rick. You're okay when you want to be."

"It's all good Mo. You already know what it is," he replied.

Mo closed the front door, took her boys by their hands and began walking towards Rick's car. She wore black stretch pants which complimented her pink tank top and fit frame. Mo knew Rick was watching her. He always watched her strut. She tied her black jacket around her waist in mid stride as she stepped aside from his view. Midway across her front yard, she looked into the vehicle they were approaching. It was a 1999 Green Montero Sport.

DeBAITed Deaths Unknown Face

Meanwhile, Jasmine spotted the parents walking towards the car with the kids. She sat up in the front passenger seat as she pulled her long wavy hair back from her face. Jasmine scanned Monique up and down, from head to toe. This was finally her time to shine.

A moment later Monique spotted Jasmine sitting in Rick's ride. *Who is this chick?* She thought. Monique stopped walking. She looked at Rick, "Who is *she*?" Mo asked.

"That's my friend Jasmine. I know you not about to trip are you Mo?" Rick speculated.

"No, I'm not, but Alex is not your son to be introducing to your *'friend'*. You should have told me this before I got out here," Monique replied as she scanned over Jasmine.

"So what, what's the problem Mo? Don't start that bullshit. Are you going to let him go or not?" Rick asked as he grew impatient.

"Please Mommy, it will be okay. I will be good." Alex interrupted.

Monique shot another quick glance at Jasmine. She answered her son, but her eyes were now locked on Rick.

"Okay sweetheart. But be ready to be back at home by eight 'o clock tonight with your little brother and be nice to Rick's friend, okay."

They felt her tone and Rick mentally dismissed the change of curfew time. Mo practically sliced Rick with her eyes. Once at the car Rick introduced Jasmine to Monique.

"Jas, this is Mo, Ashton's mother and this is Ashton and that's Alex, his brother. I am taking both of them with us."

Monique interrupted, challenging Jasmine. "Hello, Jasmine is it? Is that okay with you?"

Jasmine tapped her fingers nervously on the arm rest as she leaned closer towards the window.

She matched Monique's tone. "Sure it is. We will take care of them."

DeBAITed Deaths Unknown Face

Monique fought hard to remain calm. "Thanks, nice to meet you." she replied.

"Me too," said Jas. She smiled, rolled up the window and then turned her attention to Rick and the boys.

Monique watched them leave as she scrolled back up her driveway. She mumbled to herself, "Jasmine? Who is Jasmine?"

After their evening out, Rick dropped the boys off at home. Mo stood watching from behind her storm door in her thick pink cashmere robe. Her eyes were focused on Jasmine and her sons.

"Can I have a hug?" Jasmine asked the boys after she and Rick got them out of the SUV.

Alex and Ashton hugged the pair before running to the front door. Mo waved them off.

"Did you two have a good time?" She asked anxiously as she ran bath water for the boys.

"Yes ma'am." Alex replied sounding satisfied.

"Me too mommy, but I just kept coughing," Ashton whined.

"Why were you coughing baby? Did you forget your inhaler?"

"Yes ma'am and daddy made Ms. Jas stop smoking because it was hard for me to breathe."

"What?"

"We still had fun though mommy. We saw a 3D show and had pizza. I even beat Rick in basketball," Alex gladly added.

"Yea, well I am glad that you had a great time. Finish up your baths and then come kiss me goodnight."

She practically marched to her room. Mo made sure that she closed her door. She paced the floor as she gathered her thoughts. *How could Rick be so careless? Ms. Jas was smoking? I wonder what else happened?*

DeBAITed Deaths Unknown Face

As Rick drove to Jasmine's place, she tried to seem casual but she wanted to understand the nature of his relationship with Alex and Monique. She reached in her pocket for her cigarette lighter.

"So are we going to be getting them every other weekend?"

"I get Ash when I can. Me and Mo got an understanding. We just take it day by day. She normally starts tripping after it's been a while though."

"Does she always *make* you take Alex too?"

She asked with more emphasis in the question than she intended. He heard it too.

"What are you saying?" he asked as he glanced over to her while he turned to access the expressway.

Detecting aggravation in the atmosphere, "Nothing," Jasmine replied.

She reclined back into the passenger seat. Almost an hour later, he pulled into her driveway. He nudged her knee to wake her up.

"Jas, get up. We're at the house."

Stretching and yawning she looked at Rick. She noticed that he was still strapped in with the motor still running.

"Rick, are you coming in?" she asked.

"Nope, I got some business to handle. I might hit you up later, no promises."

"I wanted to kick it tonight Rick. I feel like getting it in." He looked her in her eyes, she smiled.

"Let me handle some business lady. I'm gone call you before I head in. Just chill for a few alright?"

"Okay, I hope so," she said as she opened the passenger door to get out.

Back at Monique's, the boys were all set for bed. They knocked on her bedroom door. "Come in," Mo beamed.

"Goodnight," the boys said drowsily as they peeped into her bedroom door.

DeBAITed Deaths Unknown Face

"Goodnight. Ash, are you feeling okay?"

"Yes ma'am," he replied.

She picked Ashton up and took Alex by his hand. Mo helped them both into bed and kissed their heads. Once she whispered prayers in their ears, she left the room. Finally, they were in bed. She needed to speak with Rick. His music blared throughout the interstate as he cruised. *'Hey let's get away. Shawty we can freak sumt'n if you down. Hey baby I was thinking of you, thinking of you.'* He was rapping the lyrics of a song by the young new artist T.I. when his cell phone rang.

"Yea." annoyed that his chill time was being interrupted as the track faded out in the background.

"Can you talk?" Mo asked.

"Yea, wassup?"

Mo snapped. "Ashton says that he had trouble breathing because "MS. JAS" kept smoking in his face after you told her not to."

Rick stood his ground. "Look woman. Do not start this shit. Every time I get Ash you complain about something. Jas lit ONE cigarette. I told her to put it out cause Ashton got asthma and she did."

"Well, if he says he was coughing then he was coughing! Rick, I don't understand why you would have anybody around that would smoke in your child's face anyway."

Rick interrupted. "Look Mo, this shit you complaining about is irrelevant. Hit me back when you get your mind right."

Mo became angrier. "Wait a minute! You tell that hood rat ass bitch to stay the hell away from my children with that hood-ghetto shit or else I will tell her!" Mo fumed as she slammed down the phone.

DeBAITed Deaths Unknown Face

Rick shook his head and turned his music back up dismissing the entire argument. He turned into the parking lot at the corner store off Bolton Road in Northwest Atlanta. He saw Chassity, Jasmine's best friend, coming out of the store. As he walked towards the door Chassity greeted him.

"What it do Rick? Where is Jas?"

"Wassup Lady? What are you doing wit' these clowns?" he replied as he scanned the faces in the car she was riding in.

Chassity knew what he was thinking. He hated her boyfriend, Orlando, and absolutely despised Naja. It was a shame that Chassity couldn't resist Orlando.

"Rick, stay in your lane and I will stay in mine."

He lit a cigarette and glared into the eyes of her boyfriend who was a conflict of interest.

"Don't let this bullshit drag you in too deep. You know your role," Rick mentioned as he exhaled.

Orlando stepped out of his car. He felt Rick's vibe, still he nodded as he walked past him to enter the store. Rick didn't respond. He remained silent as he looked over her choice of clothes. Chassity wore a skin tight, thigh high black dress, clear stilettos, with a long black weave down her back. Her beautiful, innocent, tan face was tarnished by a lip ring and the eye brow piercing was too much. The twenty two year old could pass for thirty years of age. Rick was disgusted. He flicked his cigarette into the parking lot and dismissed Chassity.

"Watcha self. Later," he instructed while reaching to catch the swinging door. Chassity had been dismissed.

Back inside of Orlando's traveling white Magnum, the smell of marijuana lingered in the air. "What's his problem?" Naja asked.

"You know how Rick is. He be on that bullshit sometimes," Chassity replied.

"Did you tell him where we were going?"

DeBAITed Deaths Unknown Face

"I didn't tell Rick anything. You know he hates both of you," Chassity reminded as she rolled her eyes at the fourth passenger, Liz, Naja's convenient partner.

"Baby, turn the music up," she requested, tuning out any further conversation with Chassity. She pulled out her compact. Liz held it while Naja snorted a line of cocaine.

Naja and Orlando, the out-casted siblings, were definitely fruit from the same tree. They understood one another. They also had all the same connections. Orlando, the half-brother of Monique and Monte, happened to also be the nark who ratted on David Carter, Rick's mob boss.

The music was blasting when Chassity answered her cell phone. "Talk to me," she greeted.

"Where you at?" asked Jasmine.

"Orlando is driving me and Naja to the Mexican restaurant on Old National Highway. Liz's lame ass is tagging along too. Wassup?"

"Nothing. We took Rick's little boy and his brother to Dave & Buster's today. So I finally saw his baby mama."

"And?" urged Chassity.

"She seemed cool, just stuck up. Do you know her? They call her Mo but her name is Monique."

Chassity was dumbfounded. *What was Rick thinking?* Chassity knew if he hadn't said anything, that she better not say anything. She had to think fast. "I can't hear you Jas. Let me call you back when I get out the car."

"Okay, cool."

She felt bad for stalling on her best friend but she had her orders.

DeBAITed Deaths Unknown Face

BRENDA

Hot-lanta steamed as the evening heat lingered at 97 degrees. Brenda Carter sashayed across the parking lot with her loaded briefcase. She loved counseling and overseeing children at the Community Center where she was Chief Director. For her it was more of a get-a-way from her real life and all the drama surrounding her husband. She often battled with the demons in her marriage. Most days she operated in a trance, yet almost every evening her mind wandered while depression settled in the pool of her tears. She resented David's playboy reputation. Most of their relationship was based on manipulation, yet still she had too much pride to walk away from her infamous husband. She sat in her car before leaving the parking garage, indecisive about keeping her plans for the evening. These days with David incarcerated, she had just grown tired and careless.

She'd lost all respect for David once she discovered Naja had been hired as his criminal defense lawyer.

She had been well acquainted with Naja. She knew of their affair years before, but David always reassured her that Naja meant absolutely nothing to him. She sat in her car staring at herself, wondering where things went wrong in their relationship. He had even fathered another child, Shelton. That time he pleaded with her to stay and she did, but Tawanna, Shelton's mother, had not made it easy to accept. Tawanna flaunted her pregnancy and used Shelton as bait to have David visit her at unusual hours. Startled by her cell phone ringing, she sighed as she viewed the caller ID.

"This is Brenda."

"Brenda, when David calls to check in, let him know that I need to speak with him regarding his son," the caller advised while chuckling at Brenda's southern accent.

DeBAITed Deaths Unknown Face

Brenda cringed at the sound of a thick, deep ghetto voice. "I am not sure when he will call. You seem to be quite friendly with his lawyer so perhaps you should have her give him the message," she sarcastically replied.

"Look, you simple dummy, don't even worry about it."

Brenda laughed. As she was in the middle of hanging up to ignore the foolishness, she heard another remark.

"Excuse me?"

"You heard me. Tell David I wanted to know if Shelton was going to live with you and him or him and Monique when I deploy. Since you don't know when he is checking in, you tell Naja to ask him that, dummy. Now how you feel?"

Before Brenda could respond, the call ended. She was stunned. Her reflection became pale. Lost in her thoughts, the pain in her chest grew heavier. The pit of her stomach began to ache. "Damn you David Carter," she whispered.

She truly felt like the dummy that Tawanna always called her. "Who in the hell is Monique?" she wailed in agony. Desperate to regain her composure, she reached into her glove compartment and pulled out a travel size bottle of grey goose vodka. With the turn of her wrist, she tossed the remedy down her throat, washing away her anti-depressants.

Heartbroken again, she sighed, "Monique." She wondered why Tawanna hated her so much. She wanted to understand why David needed Naja to be by his side.

"Why do I deal with this God? Why?" How much more can I take?" she asked herself out loud in her lonely atmosphere.

DeBAITed Deaths Unknown Face

Brenda married David after he was sentenced. Their mutual understanding was to protect their assets. She knew that David genuinely loved her and made her feel as if she was the only woman alive when he was present. Unfortunate for her, he made every woman who he made contact with feel the same way. Naja was the first woman she had ever known to rapidly gain his trust. His adoration of her was no longer enough, she needed respect.

Glancing at her digital clock on her CD player, she remembered her plans. *'Another fifteen minutes and I have to head home,'* she thought. Mrs. Brenda Carter picked up her cell phone. She pressed the '8' to speed dial, hoping Chassity would answer. The call connected. "You have reached Cha--". No answer. She clicked off her cell phone and reclined the black leather seat of her BMW forward. She then reapplied her mascara above and beneath her hazel eyes. Next, she replaced her red lipstick onto her pale lips and sprayed a refreshing fragrance between her thighs. Mrs. Carter picked up her phone to make another call. At that moment, she heard the car horn she had been anticipating. She zipped her make- up bag closed and opened her car door. His deep, sexy voice changed her mood.

"Hey Baby. I am sorry to keep you waiting."

"Not a problem. I just finished making a few phone calls," Brenda replied as she stepped out of her car.

"I'll drive tonight. My wife won't be home till after ten," Freddie replied.

Brenda faced her lover. "Sounds like cat and mouse tonight," she teased.

Little did she know she was falling into a trap set just for her own demise. She would have to swim or sink in the sea of deception.

DeBAITed Deaths Unknown Face

JASMINE

In the kitchen, Jasmine seasoned the meat for the barbecue grill. Her long, natural, wavy hair and thin build resembled Chilli from the group TLC, except her complexion was much lighter. Her beautiful hazel eyes complimented her dimples. Both of her arms were tatted with hearts and angels, portraying her religious beliefs throughout her body. Her personality glowed in her natural beauty and charming spirit. Everyone she knew loved to be around her. Chassity was also there greeting guests and helping Jasmine prepare the food.

"Can I ask you something?" Chassity quizzed.

"Girl, since when have you been shy about asking anybody anything?"

"So what is going on between you and Rick? How did that jump off?"

"Long story short, Naja put a bug in my ear about him digging me. We kicked it the other day when his baby mama let him get the boys. Later that night my ass was tossed up and he dropped that hammer." She laughed. "Seriously though, Rick has always been cool to me. He seems to be on his grown man act," Jasmine replied.

Chassity laughed too. "Well Jas, all I can tell you is to be careful. Rick ain't no joke and please believe he is serious about those boys."

"Alright, I hear ya."

Out on the patio deck, she flipped the chicken on the grill. Jas danced her favorite two steps to the music while taking a drag from her cigarette. Rick watched her as she blew the smoke into the air.

"So are you enjoying yourself?" he asked.

"You already know baby. What about you? Are you enjoying yourself?"

"Yea I am." Unexpectedly, he became serious.

"But you need to chill out with all that dancing around."

DeBAITed Deaths Unknown Face

He tilted his head and turned her chin to face him. She met his eyes. Rick's eyes always turned colors when his moods changed. Jealousy pierced through his hard demeanor.

"I think that you are moving around too much in front of these niggas." Rick's raspy voice was stern.

She felt fire shoot through her veins.

"Rick, please don't start any mess out here."

"You heard what I said," Rick advised before going back inside.

Chassity greeted Brenda at the door. "Hey boo, did you get my message?"

Brenda smiled. "Hey boo. Yes, I did. Here is the camera and a bottle of Patron. Let's take pictures before the crowd gets too deep. I don't plan to be here long."

"That's cool. DJ dropped by. He can take our pictures right quick. Oh shit, let me go get the rest of the meat off the grill." Chassity rushed away. Brenda laughed as she hugged her son.

Chassity was removing the rest of the chicken and hamburger patties from the grill when Brenda approached her.

"I need to talk to you about Tawanna and Naja."

"This is not the time or the place," Chassity stated.

"Can't this wait? Please, too many ears are here right now," Jas mentioned.

"Fine, but who is Monique?" Brenda urged for a response.

Knowing exactly which Monique was in question, Chassity pretended to not know anything at all.

"What is her last name?" she asked.

Jasmine stood silently. Her gut told her not to speak. At that moment she made a mental note to keep her ears open and her eyes wide.

"I don't know her last name yet, but if you know something you should be letting me know," Brenda requested.

DeBAITed Deaths Unknown Face

"We do not do drama over here. Let's go inside before this meat dries out. Not the time," Chassity demanded.

A while afterwards, Jasmine began putting ice into the blender to make some more daiquiris.

"Rick, where is the rum?" she asked out loud over the music. "Damn! I knew I forgot something. I got to run to the liquor store. Anybody else need anything?" Rick asked as he patted his pockets in search of his car keys. Rick called, "Let's roll Monte," who was also at the cookout.

In the car, Rick and Monte rode as they laughed about the crowd back at the house. They began to compare notes about how everybody was getting wasted, the chicken that burned, and the ladies who were there. Monte had his eyes on Brenda. She wore a yellow sundress with white, dark yellow and thin black swirls in the center of the dress and diamond accessories. Brenda was always beautiful. A classy-simple dressed lady. After meeting David, she had made a conscious decision to leave the street life alone. Completely unaware of the target on her forehead, she would soon fall victim to another bite of her enemies bait.

"Brenda is a top notch chick. I was checking her out when she and Chassity took pictures. Nice ass too," Monte mentioned.

Rick chuckled while he reached in the arm rest for his ringing cell phone. As they pulled in at the store, Rick told Monte he would catch up with him in a few minutes after his phone call.

"Hello." Rick greeted.

"Hey, where are you?"

"I'm at the store. Wassup?"

"Wassup is that you were supposed to get Ashton yesterday but you didn't. Now today we haven't heard from you," Mo snapped.

"Man, I called you last night and you didn't answer. So don't call tripping now. Plus …"

DeBAITed Deaths Unknown Face

"FIRST of all, you called me back after eleven last night." She cut him off mid-sentence. "And that's after I had called you three times!"

"Look, it ain't that serious. Stop with the bullshit Mo." Rick clutched his fist to control his temper and tone. "I'm at the store. Now is not the time to go back and forth with you Mo. Damn! If I come get him now, we won't have long to kick it since he gotta be back for school in the morning."

His words meant nothing. Monique was still pissed. "You tell him that!"

Before Rick could respond he heard his son on the phone. "Hey daddy!" he squealed. "Hey man, what cha' up to?"

"I was playing my video games. I've been reading my books and I was eating my cookies. Are you coming to get me?"

"Not today man. I want you to rest so that you will be ready for school tomorrow. Daddy will come see y'all this week, okay?"

"Okay daddy. I Love You."

"I love you too man," Rick replied trying to hide his own disappointment.

"You know you wrong for that Rick!" Mo said on the low.

He knew that she was still upset about Jasmine smoking around the boys.

"Look Mo, I'm gonna come by one day this week to visit so stop tripping. I didn't intend for everything to happen like it did."

"Whatever Rick!" were the final words he heard before she slammed down the phone.

In the store, Monte was already checking out at the counter. Rick came in and nodded at a few familiar faces. He breezed through the aisles, grabbed his items, and checked out. Once outside, he stopped to light a cigarette. Monte asked if everything was good, referring to the phone call.

"It is what it is man," Rick confided.

DeBAITed Deaths Unknown Face

"Monique?" Monte assumed.

"You already know."

Monte shook his head. Mo was his sister, but Rick was his best friend and he never got in the middle of those two.

They rode back to Jasmine's house in silence. He let his thoughts linger towards the outline of Brenda's body. He debated how he could play her into his plans for the night. Later that night, Brenda bit the bait Monte presented and just as his half-sister Naja had planned, she ended up in his bed.

DeBAITed Deaths Unknown Face

DAVID

Resting on his back, passing his time for racketeering and money laundering, David had few worries. He had all the confidence in the world that Naja would have him released and his record expunged in no time.

He married Brenda right after he became aware of the time that he was facing. At that time he had just suffered a financial loss after being set-up at one of his clubs, so he married her to stay vested until he could afford to cash out of the arrangement. He married her for every reason at the time other than love. Before his marriage to Brenda, he had already fallen in love with Monique and he dreaded confirming the fact that he did indeed get married. *'I've got to tell her that I am living a lie even behind these prison bars,'* he thought.

He knew Brenda and Monique continued to live their lives. They both frequented different men in the streets. Last winter, he called home and Brenda answered only to ask him to call back. It was the way she sounded that never settled with him. She had told him that she was in the shower, but it sounded like a little more was going on to him and he never forgot that.

When he met Mo, she was down to earth. At first, he felt that it would be too risky to deal with Monique after he found out about her connection with Rick. Unbeknownst to David, Naja set the trap for Monique to meet him. She introduced Mo as a paralegal, which at the time Mo assisted her on a temporary basis. Monique was under the impression that Naja was helping her get her life back on track. Naja had even paid her sister's tuition for her to return to school. In the beginning, Mo was excited about her new possibilities with David. Suspiciously, Naja finally told Monique her intentions for David. Monique agreed to the deceit as a way to repay her sister, yet no one ever told him that she and Naja were sisters.

DeBAITed Deaths Unknown Face

She had even convinced Monique that Rick would never know of her relationship with David. Instead, she coached Monique on how to persuade him into falling in love. Her sophistication, charming personality, and willingness to be the other woman all played beneficial roles. Needless to say, Naja was even more confident that Monique would never know she was sleeping with both David and Rick. She had everyone right where she wanted them, or so she thought. David wasn't the fool that Naja thought he was and Rick was no snitch. Within a couple of years of David dating Monique, Naja made sure that he was set up in a bad deal by an undercover informant at one of his clubs. She assumed that no one suspected Orlando to be in connection with her.

David sighed as he rose up to walk over to his wall where his pictures were taped at eye level. Brenda had sent him a picture of herself with Chassity posing at Jasmine's cookout. His eyes shifted to the next set of pictures. He gazed at his sexy Monique straddling a chair wearing only a thong and heels. At that moment his thoughts began to wonder as he pondered over the lovers in his life. *'Who can I tolerate to lose?'* He felt that Brenda had been unfaithful, but he couldn't prove it. Thanks to Brenda, David never went without the things he needed in prison to survive. She kept his business legitimate, but she kept her personal business to herself.

He left his unit to use the phone. The line connected. He heard her take a deep breath. She heard the automated system prompt her, "Press '5' now." He irritated her when he called. Brenda spoke, sounding dry, disturbed, "Hey."

"Hey Brenda," David spoke. His Italian accent lingered through the phone line. "I have a few people coming by to take care of some personal things for me. I wanted to make sure that you know to keep the safe locked and shut down all the computers, alright? You got that?"

DeBAITed Deaths Unknown Face

Brenda stirred her Merlot around in her large wine glass. She couldn't care less about what he wanted. She wanted to know *who* Monique was. "Sure. You know honey it's funny how you call the shots from prison and still continue to maintain all of your relationships. What are your plans for Monique?" Brenda accused.

David dropped his head, half holding the telephone. He knew she was throwing bait. He also knew that if his wife had details, she would be speaking facts. His deep voice was defensive. "Speak up Brenda. Spit it out."

"David, *who* is Monique?" she finally asked.

He sighed once he heard his wife call his mistress by name. He knew there was nothing more to do other than to come clean.

"B, she is someone that I know. We can't get into this now. Just handle everything and I will be in touch soon. Later." He ended the call.

Brenda held the line as the dial tone interceded the silence. At her breaking point, she threw her wine glass, crashing it against the wall.

Once he was back in his unit, he picked his mail up from his bunk. He had three letters, one from his oldest son, the second from Mo, and the final letter from his brother Anthony, his right hand man. He read Anthony's letter first. He knew it was about business:

"The numbers are in and they match...no problem. Your kids are good. Brenda's getting sloppy. The dirty cop is in too deep and the red head is out. Get ready to make some moves. Let Rick drive."

DeBAITed Deaths Unknown Face

    His spirit shifted as he cut the letter up to flush it down the toilet. He wondered if Naja *had* actually deceived him. He knew that if Rick was being called to handle his problems, things were bad. Still at the moment he knew to give things a few days. It would only be a matter of time before he got his answer. Next, he read a card from David Jr., "DJ". It was a funny greeting of a naked woman bent over the hood of the car.
The words read: *"Hood ornaments with a view."*

    Finally, he rested his head against the wall as he sat back on the bunk and read the letter from Mo. The overall letter was routine. She wrote about her hopeful emotions towards their relationship, the children, and their future. It was always the ending that held his attention.
"No matter what it is, just please tell me the truth.
Love Always, Monique"
Those words felt more like a warning, or was it just his guilt?

DeBAITed Deaths Unknown Face

BRENDA

Brenda softly purred. "Thanks slow-stroker. I needed that."

She rolled onto her stomach easing off of the body of her latest lover, Monte.

"I believe you turned me out," the young lover revealed. Brenda moved her body away from Monte. He didn't notice her check her cell phone that was tucked underneath the corner of their mattress in the quarter million dollar home David bought for her. Her cell phone screen glowed "New text message." She pressed "View." The message read: *"She leaves at nine today. Call me."*

With Freddie on her mind, she glanced at her entertainment center. The time read 3:36 am. Monte wasn't the stallion Brenda had hoped for, but he was good enough for the evening. She rolled over, nibbled his ear, and whispered, "House rules slow-stroker."

Monte reached around her waist and pulled her closer. He wanted to talk. "Brenda, we've been doing this for a while. How long will house rules rule?" he asked in the voice of a needy man.

"The house rules as long as the house belongs to me. No strings, no attachments, remember?" she reminded him as she nudged away from him and slid out of bed onto her feet.

Mrs. Carter stepped off towards the bathroom naked. Her full breast, small waist, and full bottom glowed from the shimmering body oils she wore.

"Come here," he beckoned.

Agitated that he didn't hit the spot, "For what?" she asked.

"Let me taste you," Monte begged.

"No, we're done here," she replied, before entering the bathroom.

DeBAITed Deaths Unknown Face

She turned the hot water on in the shower and yelled from the crack of the bathroom door. "Leave Monte. I will call you. I enjoyed spending the evening with you."

Before he could respond, the door slammed. He heard the click of the lock. The point was taken, so he left.

After a hot satisfying shower, she dried her body, rubbed on her lotion, and slipped on her night gown. A few hours later, she heard her cell ringing. She felt like she had just fallen asleep. Realizing that it was early morning, she thought, *Freddie!* She was disappointed when she saw the caller. She fell back onto her fluffy pillow. Irritated, she put the earpiece to her ear.

"Press '5' to accept or hang up now." She accepted out of routine and then mumbled, "Hello."

"Wassup?" David replied.

"What time is it?" Brenda asked.

"Late night?" He accused.

"Not at all," she replied.

"What's going on?" He continued before she answered.

"Have you checked on my kids?"

Brenda sat up. "The last time we spoke you hung up before I could tell you that Tawanna's ghetto ass called my phone the other day. She wanted you to know that she is going to deploy and that Shelton will need to live here since you are coming up for parole."

"What?" Tawanna deployed 6 months ago. Shelton has been living with her parents in South Georgia. He will finish the school year out down there. I thought I told you that."

His wife was agitated. "No honey, you didn't. Maybe it was Monique making the phone call. Whomever the caller was seemed just as concerned about your living arrangements as they were about your son."

"What caller Brenda?" David became suspicious. He was particular about the people he communicated with and even more particular about who communicated with his wife.

DeBAITed Deaths Unknown Face

She had his attention. "I told you. I thought it was Tawanna. They used her phone to call. She cussed me out, started telling me that you and a Monique would be living together."

David laughed. "You're silly Brenda."

"Am I?" She leaned into the receiver, screaming into the phone. "David why is it that every time you cheat, get busted, or go to jail I have to clean up your mess and clean up all of your trash that you allow to blow into our yard! I get so damn tired of being the blame. I am not crazy David Carter and I do not make these things up. I did not create a story about Shelton, Naja, Tawanna, or Monique! This is your mess David!"

Her rant left the line silent for a few moments.

"Are you done?" he asked.

She cracked the ice, "Am I done? David, I was with you years before I married you and dumb enough to take you as my husband before you went to prison. Now you want to know if I am done? Why are you asking now David? After all these years, you're asking *me* if I am done with your sorry ass? Do you think that I am going to make it easy for you to leave me? We have built a life together. Hell no! I am not done with you. And you are not done David. Am I clear? Now this Monique *person* is getting under my skin. It would be in your best interest to remove her from our lives. I am sick and tired of your indiscretions David and I will not tolerate anything else. Am I making myself clear?" Brenda demanded.

He knew she was telling the truth. He realized someone on the outside had inside information.

He became grim. "If you ever decide to use this tone with me again, *Mo* will be the least of your worries. Do you understand?" His cold voice silenced.

'Did he just call her by her nickname and defend her?' She thought.

DeBAITed Deaths Unknown Face

Before she was able to respond, she heard him hang the phone onto the receiver. Chills flushed through her body. For the first time in fifteen years she felt that her marriage and relationship with David was in serious trouble. She hung up the phone then rested her back onto her pillow. She noticed the glowing lights on her cell. The vibrations indicated a new text message. Freddie. Ah Damn! She had almost forgotten. She grabbed her cell phone. *'Don't be late'*, she read.

The time was 8:26 AM. She jumped from bed, showered again, brushed her teeth, washed her face, ran her fingers through her short styled hair, and scanned the closet for something sexy to throw on. She grabbed it. *'Screw it'* she thought. With less than twenty minutes left, she jumped into her yellow sundress, the one that she had worn only once before. Traffic from Riverdale to Avondale that time of the morning was not bad for a Saturday. She had called Freddie and told him that she was on her way. They met at one of her rental properties for a morning quickie. Around noon, he mentioned that he needed to take care of some business, "Are you up for having hot dogs at Skips?" he asked Brenda.

She agreed to have lunch at Skips, a popular hot dog shop in the heart of Avondale. Freddie was more of Brenda's speed for a companion. The sixty one year old distinguish gentlemen didn't look any older than fifty years of age. Their affair had been going on for the last three years. Freddie told Brenda that he and his wife were divorcing. Supposedly, his agreement with his wife was to be cordial until the proceedings were final.

Just as the pair took their seats, a bus of 6-10 year olds pulled up to celebrate their softball win. He saw them first. *No*, he thought. Seconds later Ashton yelled, "Grandpa!" "Grandpa, we won the game!" Alex shouted.

DeBAITed Deaths Unknown Face

Monique hadn't told him that she would have the boys or else he would not have brought Brenda. He didn't like the risk of them saying anything to their Grandma.

Freddie didn't know what to expect. There didn't *seem* to be an emergency. *'Oh goodness'* he thought. Brenda, clueless of course, sat quietly as the two adorable boys hugged their Grandpa. Another quick second, she was there too. Brenda continued to observe as a jazzy, fit, young female spoke to Freddie.

"Hi Daddy. Who is your friend?"

Freddie was quick on his feet. "Hey baby girl. This is Ms. Jones."

Brenda sat patiently, understanding his need for discretion.

"This is my daughter, Tootsie. " Freddie informed Brenda.

Mo smiled before she excused herself. "I need to order their food and we can speak later, since you have company."

"That will be fine. We will sit with the boys until you get back, then we have to head out of here." Freddie replied.

Moments later Mo returned. "Thanks Daddy. Let's take a few pictures before they eat these messy hotdogs. We need to frame this celebration," Mo smiled.

Freddie looked at Brenda, she smiled and nodded. It seemed innocent enough. Mo had requested Coach Brad to take a few shots.

"Well, we gotta go," Freddie announced as he hugged his grandsons and daughter.

"Nice to meet you Ms. Jones," Monique mentioned.

"You too, take care," Brenda politely responded.

The boys enjoyed their meal with the team while Monique watched her dad leave with Brenda.

DeBAITed Deaths Unknown Face

Outside, Freddie wondered why Mo had told him that she had to meet him there at noon. "What was so important?" But he didn't mention it to her. He and his companion would know soon enough just how much bait they had bitten off.

DeBAITed Deaths Unknown Face

DAVID

He counted during his work out, "One-set, two-set, and three-set".
"MAIL CALL!" yelled the guard.
"…Eight-set, nine-set, ten."
"CARTER!" the guard yelled.
David pumped his chest after he stood to his feet. Adjusting his eyes, he focused to see the lavender colored envelope the guard was handing him. Mo. He knew it before he flipped the envelope over to read the senders name. The package felt thick. Inside, he had a romantic card, a letter, and pictures. The first picture was of Ashton, Alex, and DJ. Although DJ was his oldest son with Brenda, he was mature enough to understand the relationship that his parents had. After a few months of dating Monique, "D" introduced his mistress to David Jr. as a friend. Over the years, Mo and DJ grew fond of one another. Whenever DJ could, he'd drop by to visit Monique. She always welcomed him and encouraged him to stay on track in his father's absence. David decided to read the letter first. He scanned over a couple of pictures. This sort of mail bored him a little, but he was always interested to hear what Monique had to say.

Mo's letter read:
> *Hey Baby, the countdown continues. You have a few weeks till your parole hearing. Everyone is doing fine. I just decided to drop you a few lines. Call me after you see the pictures.*
> *Love You*

DeBAITed Deaths Unknown Face

In conclusion the letter read:

P.S. Daddy still thinks he is a pimp. Check this out. He knows his divorce with mama isn't final, but he is already showing off his new lady. A couple of weeks ago, the boys won their softball tournament, so the coach took all the teams to Skips for hotdogs. We weren't in there five minutes before Ash and Alex spotted daddy with another woman.

By the time he was finished reading Mo's letter he was laughing out loud for the moment. Sitting at the edge of his bunk, he thumbed through the pictures. He read each caption on the back.

"The boys being silly"... "At the park"... "Leaving Six Flags." Midway through the stack, he saw something in one picture that made him flip back to that picture. He turned it over first. The caption read: *We won the game. Me posing with the boys at Skips. Daddy and Ms. Jones booed up at Skips.*

Ms. Jones *was Brenda.* In a state of shock he flipped the picture over. He stared at the photo. Anxiety grew in the pit of his stomach. He had a feeling that his bowels were going to take over his body. "Oh Shit!" he yelled. Tears of hurt, pride, and anger swelled in his eyes. All the other photos fell onto the floor along with the card, letter, and the envelope. He walked over to his board, the place where he displayed all of his photos. He compared the picture of Ms. Jones next to Mrs. Carter. "Brenda Jones Carter! You cheating ass bitch. That's your ass now!" He growled as he mashed in her face on the picture with his thumb.

In the photo with Mo and her family, Brenda wore a yellow sundress with white, dark yellow, and thin black swirls. The EXACT same dress she wore in a picture with Chassity at Jasmine's cookout not too long ago.

DeBAITed Deaths Unknown Face

His thoughts trailed off... "DAMN! Think, think, think 'D'", he whispered to himself. Weigh your options."
Mo has to understand. She knows I was with Brenda. She just doesn't know that we're married. He thought about the connection between his wife and his mistress. He could not believe that his wife was sleeping with the father of his mistress. "Damn! Brenda has my cars, money, house, access to all my accounts. Plus, she has all of my business information." He shook his head. Unbelievable! He finally spoke what he thought made sense. "I need Mo." He called; she answered.

"Press 5 now or hang up." She pressed 5.

"Hey honey. Did you get your mail today?" Mo asked.

He played it cool. "I sure did. Thank you for everything that you do. You have really shown me a lot these last few years. I just want you to know that I Love You Monique."

Mo was suspicious. She knew Brenda. Brenda just didn't know her. She knew he saw the picture. She decided to remain silent about it. She put her sweetest voice to work. "Awe, I love you too. I know your time gets the best of you, but don't worry, everything is going to be alright. Baby, since you are coming back to Atlanta soon, you have to talk to Brenda. Should I even be trying to resume our wedding plans considering your date has been set?"

Damn! He hated when she backed him into a corner. "What have I been telling you Mo?"

She was amused. Monique had him right where she wanted him. "I just want to make sure David. I was just being clear about the things I've heard you say. I also read what you write on paper, but I just need to know if you are really ready. Are you really *able* David? Are you really in a position to marry me?" She gave him his bait. He could take it or leave it.

He left the bait. "Yes Mo. I am willing, ready, and able to finally marry you. I love you."

That day he lost her respect. "Love you too," Monique responded.

Back at his bunk, he whispered to himself, "I didn't think Brenda had it in her." He was truly shocked, lost in his thoughts. *'Dumb enough to cheat on me, but smart enough to fool with an older cat and use her maiden name.'* He began to realize that he may have underestimated his wife.

He knew that if at least six people used the phone after him, that the thirty minutes to make another phone call had expired. Hell, at this point he had more to lose with Brenda. He figured that he and Mo could negotiate, considering her discretions since his incarceration. He planned to use all those things against her if he had to. He figured Mo was good for now. If he did lose Brenda or his possessions, he anticipated that Monique would step right in.

Finally, he was able to call Brenda. "Press 5 now or hang up."

Brenda accepted the collect call. "Hey."

"Hey, what's up?" David responded. "What's going on? Has anyone been over on business?"

She rolled her eyes before responding. "Yes, he was over the other day."

"Good. So what else is going on?" David asked, not really expecting a confession.

She could barely stand to talk to him. "What do you mean? Since when do you give a damn? Funny you haven't *been* asking what's going on. So what is supposed to be going on David?"

He heard her guilt. "Look, I didn't call you for all that. Call my lawyer and tell her to tie up my loose ends by Friday."

"Okay." Brenda agreed but dismissed the message. She wanted some questions answered. "So what are you planning to do once you are out?"

DeBAITed Deaths Unknown Face

He wasn't interested in any further conversation. "I have kids. My first priorities are my kids and then I have to get a job. I'll be out on parole."

She chuckled. At that point, she was convinced that he had plans of living with another woman. David never had a job, much less looked for one. "Then what?" insinuated Brenda.

"Then nothing, time will reveal the rest." He paused.

She knew he wouldn't explain. She had to go. She interrupted. "I have to go David, so bye."

"Later," he replied and ended the call.

After the evening inmate count down, David decided that he needed to come up with a plan if all else failed. The one person he did not want to lose or felt that he could not lose was Monique. David's thoughts drifted into a daze. I have to be able to trust the lady that I close my eyes on. Now I need to know Mo's every move till I get home. "Damn!" He yelled audibly. He almost forgot about Freddie, Monique's Dad. Thinking of how to handle things, he made his list.

He decided it was time to write Ant back using private terminology.
"It's hot at the house and I need to move
everything before it blows. I got a favor that is due, so wait for it to come to you. Move fast. This can't wait.
We will talk soon. Stand your post. The whole game is about to change."

He never signed his letters. Feeling more at ease, he made his next move in his second letter.

DeBAITed Deaths Unknown Face

He wrote: "Make sure the right person gets this. Six hundred dollars says that if she stays until she gets the signal to go that it will be long enough. He crossed the line interfering business with pleasure. It's all good because it will become a benefit. Ride the waves and do what you are supposed to do. Never lose focus. Things may happen that you do not understand. Call DJ and tell him to fall back on visiting Mo for a while. Fill in all gaps. Lock my accounts with the personal PIN in the safe deposit box. Move the escrow account over. I've had our banker notified. You have all access until I am released.   I can't afford for anything to happen to either of you. I've been betrayed and it will only get worse. Later."

He sealed each letter and then mailed them three days apart to prevent everyone from making obvious moves at the same time.

DeBAITed Deaths Unknown Face

JASMINE

Crying hysterically with the cordless phone to ear, Jasmine just kept screaming in agony.

"What! No, No! Why? Oh my GOD, NOOOO!!!!! Please don't lie to me!"

Rick rushed to her side. He took the phone from her hand. "I got her. Just call back. Jasmine has fallen on the floor. Just call back," he said into the receiver.

She continued to cry out, "Poor baby, poor, poor innocent baby."

"Calm down baby," Rick whispered. "Tell me what happened. Who was that on the phone?"

Sniffling and still crying, she cried, "It's about my sister. Tawanna was killed in Iraq this morning. She's dead. Oh my God! How are we going to tell Shelton his mommy is dead?"

At a loss for words, Rick held Jasmine close to his chest. He actually felt for her. He let his silent tears fall over her head.

Jasmine relocated to Atlanta after she ran into trouble in South Georgia. She had only shared pictures with Rick of her nephew Shelton with his mom, Tawanna.

"Who was on the phone?" Rick repeated as he held Jasmine tightly and rocked her back and forth.

She coughed as she struggled to speak. "Mama was on the phone. Tawanna was killed in Iraq. The jeep she was in was hit by a bomb. It killed all three passengers. She deployed a couple of months before I met you."

He rubbed her back until she cried herself to sleep, then he carried her to her bed, laid her down and closed the door.

Rick plopped down on the couch. The news stressed him. He had never lost a sibling, but he knew the pain Jasmine felt. He felt for Alex like that after he lost his dad, Mike. "Damn!" Rick yelled as he reached across the table for his cigarette lighter.

DeBAITed Deaths Unknown Face

He lit his comfort before picking up Jasmine's phone to scan for Chassity's number. He stopped at Brenda's name but decided against it, wanting to steer clear of any conversation regarding Monte. Finally, he highlighted Chassity's name and pressed the call button. No answer, only her voice mail. He pressed '1' to send a numeric page. Twenty minutes later, Chassity returned the call.

"Hello," Rick greeted.

Chassity greeted back sarcastically, "Oh hell naw! Damn nigga. Y'all ain't married. How you gone be answering my folk's phone? Where the hell they do that at?"

He ignored her words. "Look man, this ain't the time. I'm calling you 'cause Jas just found her sister got killed."

"NOT TAWANNA!" Chassity screamed. "Awe damn! I'm on my way!"

A half hour later, Chassity pulled up with her dude, Orlando, Naja and Liz. In the house, Chassity ran down the hall to Jasmine's bedroom. She saw Jas lying there in the fetal position crying quietly as she thought about the horrible news. She curled up behind her friend and cried with her.

"I'm here," Chassity whispered. "Brenda is on the way too."

Meanwhile, out on the patio, Rick rolled him a blunt. Orlando came out to smoke the marijuana that had been rolled. Naja and Liz came out soon after to start the grill. Once the grill was going, Naja and Liz went inside to prepare the meat. Orlando discussed the situation with Rick. He reminisced in Rick's presence with a few other guys.

"Dis' kinda situation ain't neva' easy," Orlando spoke. He sounded ignorant when he spoke, yet his demeanor required people to respect him, except for Rick. Orlando would forever be nothing more than a snitching punk as far as he was concerned. Rick smoked as he watched the scene. Everyone he needed to have tabs on was there.

DeBAITed Deaths Unknown Face

"Shit, I guess it's time to switch it up a lil bit," Orlando announced as he left to speak to a dude who he recognized.

In his youth his dangerous past led him to serve fifteen years in a state penitentiary. Soon he would face recent drug related charges. Orlando maintained an attitude of arrogance. His connections were strong and he too has his role in Naja's plan to take the Carters for everything they were known for. The half-siblings masterminded the plan of resentment. They never had anything so they simply wanted to take it from someone else. They had a sense of entitlement that was fueled by resentment and greed and they would mercilessly use and destroy anyone who stood in their way.

As the word spread about Jas' sister, more friends began to drop by. Jasmine was known for partying. She wasn't loose; she just liked to have a good time. She grew up in a tight knit family, one sister, and four older brothers. As a teenager, she was convicted of trafficking cocaine and possession of a firearm. Now she had finally left the troubles of her past in the past.

Chassity spoke from Jasmine's bathroom door. "I ran you some bath water Jas, so go take a bath and I will go make sure these freeloaders ain't trying to rob you."

"Just chill today, Chassity, no drama. Please, just chill okay?"

"Okay gurl," Chassity agreed as she peeped out of the blinds from Jas' bedroom. "The mail man just dropped the mail. You want me to get it?"

"Yea, you or Rick, that's it. I'll be up front when I get out of the tub."

DeBAITed Deaths Unknown Face

"Okay", Chassity replied. As she walked down the hall towards the front of the house, she noticed Rick on the patio smoking with Monte. She watched their communication while they poked at the meat on the grill. She saw "O" talking to some random dude. Who is he? she wondered. She had on a head scarf tied in the front of her head. Her weave was matted and tangled on her back. She wore a clean white tank top, some purple sweat pants with the word "Juicy" printed in white letters fitting across her butt, with some grey socks and black slippers. She took the mail from Jasmine's mailbox. She saw mail from David, but as she glanced around, she saw Brenda approaching her so she hid the letter. Brenda walked with Chassity into the house.

"You look a damn mess," Brenda said as she hugged Chassity.

Jasmine approached them in the living room. Chassity handed her the mail.

"How are you feeling?" Brenda asked.

"I just can't believe my sister is gone. I just wanna get wasted," she sighed as they hugged.

"When are you going home?" Chassity asked.

Jas answered as she pulled her hair back into a pony tail. "Maybe tomorrow. I got to see if Rick will take me, unless you feel like driving."

Chassity's mind was elsewhere and she sounded distracted. "Just do what's best for you, okay?"

"Where is Rick?" Jasmine asked.

Chassity was anxious to leave the room. "He is on the patio with Monte, Naja and Liz," she replied as she got up.

Now, standing in the dining area, Chassity could see every angle of the three bedroom town home. She scanned over the crowd in the front yard, then to the crowd that was eating on the patio. She thought to herself, *'Naja has slept with damn near everybody here.'*

DeBAITed Deaths Unknown Face

"Stop being mean. It's written all over your face," Brenda teased Chassity.

"Let me put this mail up. Y'all meet me in the kitchen and pop one of them bottles. Let's get to it," Jasmine ordered.

They giggled. Brenda and Chassity took seats at the kitchen table. Brenda kept her voice low as she expressed her views on the latest chain of events.

"Now, I never expected this. Too much has been going on lately. David just called last night and now this. I am not sure how he is going to take the news. After all, Tawanna was his son's mother. And poor Shelton, I just can't imagine how heavy his sweet little heart is dealing with this."

"I know right." Chassity began speaking. "This just blew my mind too. And what is up with you and Naja? Why you didn't speak to her? Ain't she still *your husband's* lawyer?" Chassity teased. "I know y'all don't still hate each other 'cause you caught her at the Super 8 with "D" like forever ago."

Brenda resumed her position. She hated when Chassity brought up the past. "His name is David. "D" is the hood, street name these whores gave him, and I couldn't care less about her. Why would you even bring that up right now? That is so tacky Chassity. Really?" as she shifted her eyes in Naja's direction.

Chassity smirked as she watched Brenda rant. She baited her. "There you go looking down your nose at her. You ain't no different. Word is that you got Monte digging in your pot with both hands!"

Brenda was embarrassed by the news. "Shhh! Shut up! *Where* did you get that from?"

"Everybody knows your name. You are Mrs. David Carter, aka Mrs. Kingpin, right? That is you ain't it?"

Jas interrupted, "I should have known you two would be in here carrying on something terrible."

DeBAITed Deaths Unknown Face

Although Jasmine's late sister Tawanna slept with David, the affair never interfered with the friendship Brenda had with Jas. Back in the day, Jasmine moved to the city and into a shelter in downtown Atlanta. She had run away from home and at the time Brenda was volunteering as a mentor. Jasmine looked up to Brenda. She had always been grateful for her taking her under her wings.

"Do you have any word on how Shelton is doing?" Brenda asked.

Jas shook her head from side to side. She didn't. She felt sad, especially for her nephew. Rick approached the kitchen, Jas stood up. When he arrived, he pulled her into his arms.

"You okay baby?" he whispered.

Brenda watched as she thought to herself, *'What's really going on?'*

Jas didn't answer as she pressed her body into Rick. When she reached to wrap her arms around his neck, she felt the letter crumble in her pants. She had almost forgotten.

"Oh yea Chassity, this is for you," she said as she pulled the letter that David had written from her sweat pants.

"What is it?" Chassity asked as she scanned the room.

Jasmine turned to make eye contact with her friend.

"Mail. I thought you said you had a P.O Box?"

"I do," Chassity confirmed as she dismissed herself. "I'm about to go home. I have to put on some clothes and I'll be back in a few hours."

Chassity called out onto the patio, "O" is y'all ready? I gotta go put some clothes on."

"Yea," Orlando replied.

Before Orlando left he embraced his half-brother, Monte. Rick watched them as he smoked his cigarette. Naja and Liz trailed in behind Orlando. Naja noticed Brenda. Her jealousy of Brenda caused her to act out whenever she was in her presence.

DeBAITed Deaths Unknown Face

Naja announced, "I'm coming back with Chassity. Hang in there Jas, and Rick we have business to discuss later, so expect a call," she stated as she glared at Brenda.

Brenda glared back and raised her eyebrow.

Liz hugged Jasmine a little longer than necessary. "I'm sorry for your loss," she whispered.

Orlando spoke softly into Jasmine's ear as he pushed some money into her back pocket. "Put deez duckets on yo' trip back home lil mama."

"Thanks Orlando," Jasmine stated as she glanced to see Rick's expression.

Rick watched as he lit another cigarette.

Chassity made a mental note of it all.

DeBAITed Deaths Unknown Face

MONIQUE

The traffic in downtown Atlanta was horrible. Monique had just heard the evening news on her car radio. Each deceased soldier would lie in state by the end of the week. Frustrated with traffic, she took a quick left off Spring Street headed for GA I-85 north. She prayed to catch Naja before she left the law firm. She pressed "send" again. Still trying to get her call through, she stressed to herself. "Damn voicemail! Why isn't her cell on? We have got to talk. This is not happening, not now! Naja please answer the damn phone!" Finally she heard silence on the line then a recording.

"Please wait while your party is located." After a few seconds the line began to ring. On the third ring Naja answered. "I was just thinking about you."

Monique was practically screaming. "I am not surprised. I have been trying to reach you all day. I heard about Tawanna!"

Naja mumbled in low tone, "Simmer yourself. We can't go there at the moment. I just got back from seeing that client yesterday."

Catching the drift of her tone, she lowered her voice. "Is someone with you?"

Naja rubbed her fingers through Rick's hair before she responded to get his attention.

"Oh it's just Bradley. We just drove into the state. I'll have to get back with you tomorrow morning."

Frustrated by the game, Monique replied, "No. This can't wait. David will probably be calling soon. This unexpected tragedy may ruin everything and we must meet tonight."

Naja completely dismissed Mo's efforts. "I see, not a problem. I should be able to fit you in around eleven, Okay?" "I'll call you at ten o'clock tonight, so make sure you pick up." Mo pressed the end button.

DeBAITed Deaths Unknown Face

"Why did you tell her you were with *Bradley*?" Rick asked.

"You know why." Naja couldn't flat out tell Monique that she was with Rick, so she lied to her like she had done on many other occasions.

Naja had left town the day before to meet with the parole board. Once she returned, she contacted Rick to move one hundred-thirty keys of cocaine. They met with their partners, cashed out some deals, and headed back to the city. Naja laughed about the games. "Besides, I couldn't think of anything else at the time."

He shook his head in disbelief. "What did she want?"

"I am not at liberty to say," she replied. She loved joking around, playing on people's emotions. Rick kept watch out of the window as she continued to drive. She rubbed her hand through Rick's thick, curly crew cut again. Her blue eyes matched his.

"Business as usual?" she asked.

"Nah, we done with that," Rick dismissed.

"Typical, one call from that bitch and you go limp," Naja insulted.

Rick remained calm. He knew that Naja hated Monique. Monte kept him in the loop on their family drama. He understood Naja's pain, as he too grew up without his natural parents. Still Naja's resentment was personal.

Back in the day her parents were indebted to Freddie who at the time owned a car lot. Naja's biological dad had been murdered during a crap game and her mother gained his debt after his death. Eventually her mother started to pay Freddie sexually. Naja always remembered seeing Freddie around their house and she despised him for making her mom do tricks for him. He used her and introduced her to heroin. Not long after she lost her father, she lost her mom due to her drug addiction. She always felt that Freddie arranged to raise her out of guilt, not love. She never told anyone that she paid

DeBAITed Deaths Unknown Face

her mother's balance. Nevertheless, Rick knew this trip couldn't be like all the other trips. He had his orders.

She didn't appreciate his rejection. "Look Rick, I know that this is a dangerous game but no one expected Tawanna to be killed. There is a lot of money at stake, almost twenty-two million dollars. Now the only person who could possibly walk with that cash is that bitch Brenda. I have invested too many years into this to let that money slide out of my hands. Listen to me. David has another hearing coming up. The parole board will consider time served. Don't panic on me now. Trust me. I know "D" and I know Mo. He really believes that she is clueless of his entire life and aside from my affair with you, I haven't kept anything from Monique. Look at us baby, we are finally together. I am tired of playing charades with Liz. David is finally ready to leave Brenda to be with Monique. We are all in the money. My plan worked. All of this has not been for nothing. Brenda is out and now so is Tawanna."

He glanced out the passenger rear view mirror then back to her within a second. Mentally, he had changed gears. His mind was focused on his mission. He tried to warn her as best he could without exposing too much information.

"This wasn't supposed to happen like this and none of this shit is going down right. Now it's getting out of hand. I told you never to underestimate any position." He exhaled and spoke as he finished smoking. "Brenda is married to the boss. He married her because he can trust her with his money. It ain't about love, sex, and games. That shit is for tricks like you and Mo."

Naja laughed hysterically. "Men!" she said and began laughing again.

He looked over at her. "What is it that I don't know?" he demanded.

He hated Naja. The only reason he sexed her was to keep an eye on her. That was part of his position.

DeBAITed Deaths Unknown Face

She finally spoke up. "I have the power to control David's fate. Monique hangs on my every word and if you listen to me, I will make sure we are all taken care of. Losing is not an option Rick."

She took her eyes off the road for a split second. Wham! Rick slapped her.

The impact of the blow caused her to lose control of the car. She managed to maneuver off to the side of the road. "You bastard! What did you hit me for?" she screamed.

Rick looked at her one last time before he shot her three times in the center of her head. His mission was complete.

* * * * * * * *

Meanwhile, Mo picked up the boys from afterschool. Unable to focus on anything, she chose a hot bath. She admired her smooth mocha skin in the mirror. Her tattoo, "M&M," right above her left hip held her attention. "Damn" she sighed. Mo blinked away the past. With one foot almost in the bath tub she heard a knock at the bathroom door.

"Yes?" she anxiously inquired.

"Mommy, the phone is for you and I already pressed 5," Alex proudly announced.

Mo reached for the phone. "Thanks. Hey baby," she greeted.

"Wassup?" David replied

She was careful not to sound questioning. "I am stepping into the bathtub as we speak. How are you? You didn't call me this morning."

David was distant. His mind was elsewhere. "Yea, I know. There was a fight at breakfast. They just lifted the lockdown."

"I miss you," she purred.

David sounded very serious. He caught her off guard. "I need you to come see me."

DeBAITed Deaths Unknown Face

"When?" Mo gasped.

"This weekend. I love you Mo." David ended the call.

She clicked the off button and sank down in the tub. She couldn't think or feel anything. She could only stare around the bathroom floor. Her stomach felt very uneasy. A tear dropped as a cold chill rushed over her body. The telephone rang right back. It scared her. Still nervous, she answered, nearly relieved to hear Chassity's voice.

"Wassup Mo?"

"What's going on stranger?"

Chassity sounded upbeat. "I guess it has been a minute huh?"

Mo knew that if Chassity was lurking around, that somewhere, something was going down.

"Yes it has. Did you find a job yet?"

Although she too was currently working for David, Chassity said, "Nope, I really haven't been looking."

Mo exhaled. "It must be nice not to worry about working or looking," as she wondered to herself what was really going on.

Chassity began to confide. "It's not like that. I've just been so stressed lately. Too much has been going on. Today I went by Mom's to pick up the rest of my bags. I wanted to talk to her but that chick went the hell off on me."

"How so?"

Chassity's attention was on her surroundings. "I don't know. She started about church and how I am a candidate for hell, I need deliverance, and blah, blah, blah. I just get so tired of hearing that all the time."

Mo participated in the game she suspected Chassity of playing. "What? Are you serious?"

"Gurl yes. I told her that my relationship was serious with Orlando."

Mo began giggling. "Did you call him Orlando or Lil Oozy?" Chassity giggled too.

DeBAITed Deaths Unknown Face

"Are you going to be okay?" Mo asked. She heard sniffles. "Hello?"

Chassity began putting in overtime for this one. "Everything is just too much Mo! I am tired of these streets and I'm tired of the game. It seems like every time I go anywhere, that somebody has something over my head. Everything is just too much and now I can't breathe. I... I just feel like I'm losing my mind sometimes!"

"How has Orlando been treating you?" Mo asked.

Mo knew her half-brother was a real piece of work. She had only heard of their relationship. Monique wanted to tell Chassity the truth about Orlando but Naja candidly expressed that if any harm was done it was too late regarding Orlando's private life as an in the closet homosexual man.

"Not always good but what else is out there for me? I've already gone through everything with him. Now he has taken all my money out the bank. Do you have any money for a few days?" Chassity baited.

"Money? How much money Chassity?"

"A couple of hundred," Chassity carefully stated. "I wanna go out of town with my friend. Her sister died and I just want to be with her."

"Awe dang, I'm sorry to hear that. Was it anyone that I know?"

"I doubt it. She isn't from around here."

Mo became very suspicious. "How do you know her then?"

Chassity was almost where she needed to be. "Damn Mo! I know other people other than you and these folks in the hood. Are you going to let me borrow some money or not?"

Mo joked, "Girl you better hurry up and get a job if all you want to borrow is a couple of hundred dollars. I'll let you borrow a hundred. Come by here tomorrow and get it. Just give it back to me when you get yourself together."

DeBAITed Deaths Unknown Face

Chassity persisted, "Okay, but can I please come get it tonight? I am not sure if we're leaving out later or early in the morning."

Mo yawned. "Well, call me when you find out when y'all leave and we will take it from there, okay?"

Chassity clocked out. "Okay, and thanks Mo."

"Talk to you later." Mo ended the call. She placed the phone on the floor beside her garden tub, lifting the drain with her toes.

Back on the highway, a few miles behind the parked Ford Focus, Rick jumped into his ride. Once inside he climbed into the back seat. He pulled the tab to access the trunk. He took a black bag from the trunk and tossed it up front. Finally, he replaced the middle seat back into place then hopped into the front seat.

"Did you make the call?" he asked.

"Yea, she told me to call her when I find out what time I am leaving," Chassity replied. "You see it?"

"Yea, I gotcha."

See you in a few," she replied.

She wore a black baseball cap with her hair tucked underneath a stocking cap. She was hidden behind dark shades as she maneuvered the large truck behind the disabled vehicle. Only one car had passed them since they pulled up behind the focus. Rick was unconcerned because he had others looking out for the authorities. He grabbed the bag and jumped out before the truck completely stopped. He grabbed the wire-tap from under his seat, wiped down the inside of the car, took her cell phone, and jumped into the truck. Chassity was already pulling off as he jumped back into the car seconds later. He took Chassity's cell phone, the one she used to call Mo, removed the SIM card from Naja's phone, tossed their phones, the wire-tap, and the gun in the bag.

They drove a few miles before swapping cars.

DeBAITed Deaths Unknown Face

By nightfall, Chassity had ordered a new cell phone. By a little after nine that night, Rick was making love to Jasmine. Chassity was at Orlando's. He always urged her to perform oral sex on him. It never occurred to Chassity that he was accustomed to prison sex. Around a quarter before eleven, Chassity called Mo again. This time, she called the house phone.

Mo answered, "Hey."

"Are you sleeping?" Chassity asked.

Mo ignored her question. "Uh, are you coming tonight or in the morning?"

"I won't have a ride till tomorrow."

Mo was relieved. "Okay, well call me when you get a ride."

Realizing the time, Mo had forgotten to call Naja. The fact that her sister had not called her made her very uneasy. She began to speed up her conversation with Chassity.

"Oh girl, I didn't know it was this late. Call me tomorrow and let me know, okay?"

"Okay." Chassity ended the call.

Mo reached and grabbed her cell phone from the bottom of the bed. She leaped to her feet to check for missed calls. That's strange, she thought. She had one missed call almost an hour prior from an unknown caller. She tried Naja's phone numerous times. The busy tone was steady each time. She felt panicky and she began to pace the floors of her house. She felt like something was going down. Chassity was calling too much. David wanted to see her. Tawanna was killed unexpectedly. Now she couldn't reach Naja. She began speed walking down the hall to look in on her boys. They were safe, both sound asleep. She thought about making a drink to relax her nerves. "Think, think, think," she whispered. She became more anxious, worried, and nervous. She grabbed her cordless phone.

DeBAITed Deaths Unknown Face

BOOM, BOOM, BOOM! Someone knocked at the door. She gasped so hard that she farted and almost screamed. "Yes, who is it?"

He leaned towards the door. "It's me, Pops. Open up Monique. I am with the Police!"

"*The police?*" Mo questioned.

She debated whether or not to run out the back door. Had it not been for the boys she would have bolted. She scurried towards the door.

"I'm coming Pops!" She peeked out of her peep hole. She saw the blur of two black faces and one white face.

"Just a second," she called as she removed the chain lock, flipped the dead bolt back and unlocked the door knob. She gradually exhaled as she pulled the door open. "Pop, what are you doing here? What's wrong?"

The white cop interjected. "I'm Officer Pease. I am with the Fulton County Sheriff's Department. May we ask you some questions?"

Before she answered she shifted her eyes past Freddie and the local cop. She had to warn him that her sons were home. If they saw him, his cover would be blown.

"Who are you? Please, my children are asleep."

"I am homicide Detective Montavious "Monte" Shafer of the Glynn County Sheriff's Department," he answered as he flashed his badge.

She crumbled her forehead. She knew him better than anyone. Still she didn't understand why he was there too. She looked at their father. Confused and shocked she asked randomly, "Homicide? Glynn County? What is this about? What has happened? Is it Rick?"

"May we come inside?" Officer Pease asked.

Mo was wearing her favorite thick pink cashmere robe. She pulled it closed tighter around her neck. She consented as she stepped to the side.

DeBAITed Deaths Unknown Face

"My children are asleep," she mentioned again. Once inside her home, she guided the men into her dining area.

She sat at the head of table in one of the matching black chairs that surrounded the rectangular glass table. Freddie took the seat at her right. He positioned his angle to be close to her. Officer Pease sat to her left. Detective Shafer leaned in the door way that separated the kitchen from the dining area. He already knew how she was going to react.

"What is going on? Somebody say something!" Mo demanded in a frustrated tone.

Freddie spoke up. "It's your sister baby.... Naja. Baby they found her ... dead. She's dead Mo."

The room was quiet as if her father had never spoken a word. The room was still. Mo inhaled, she didn't move. Her body hit the floor, she fainted. Her sister, her partner in crime, the woman who she trusted to fix her future was now dead.

* * * * * * * *

"Is she okay?" Mo could hear mumbles of concern as her blurred vision danced in her eyes.

"Is she okay?" Maybe we should just let them take her in Freddie."

"M- Ma- Mama, Mo began to slur. Mama Nooo!!!!"

Painful tears streamed down Monique's face. Her heart was heavy. Lying on her back she stared up from her couch into the faces of Officer Pease, Detective Shafer, Pop, and the Emergency Crew Technicians,

"She will be okay," she heard one of the EMT's announce. The other one checked her vitals. "She's stable, just keep her hydrated." The two EMTs left.

Her mother Lily was at her side holding the hand of her only child. "Oh Monique baby, mama is here."

DeBAITed Deaths Unknown Face

The voice of her sweet mother caused her to sob even harder. "It's going to be okay." Her mom continued to soothe her. The telephone began to ring. The sound of the phone woke her son Alex. He walked from his room into the living room. "Grandma?" he called still drowsy from his slumber.

"Alex." Freddie called as he rushed to block the scene.

Before Alex could focus, Freddie carried him back to bed. "What's wrong with mommy?" he asked.

"Aw she is fine. Don't you worry. Let's get you back to sleep, okay?" His grandpa stayed with him as he fell asleep.

"Freddie?" his wife called as she peeked into Alex's door leaving Mo on the couch and with the browsing officials observing the home.

"Yes," he whispered as he pulled from Alex's bed, tip-toeing to the door with his index finger covering his lips. Outside the closed bedroom door the couple stood face to face.

"We can take the boys with us," Lily, his wife suggested.

"They have school...tomorrow is Friday," Freddie debated.

"Oh, one day won't hurt for them to miss. Besides, there is too much going on. They don't need to hear or see everything."

"You're right" he agreed, "but what about Tootsie?"

"Chassity just called. She said that she will come over to stay with Monique."

"Chassity? Who is that?"

"Monique tutored Chassity in her junior and senior year of high school. Naja introduced them. She was Monique's first student the summer she received her degree."

"I don't think I know who she is."

"That doesn't surprise me. Back then you were busy learning other names, but that is neither here nor there. I know Chassity. She has become a dear friend to Monique. They will be fine."

DeBAITed Deaths Unknown Face

Freddie entered the living room. Mo's parents then informed her that the boys would be spending the weekend with them.

"Someone named Chassity is coming over to stay with you," Freddie mentioned.

"Chassity? Who called *Chassity*?" Mo asked,

Detective Shafer interrupted, "She called here."

Officer Pease supported the statement. "I answered the call and handed the phone to your mother."

Mo raised her head and slammed her feet down as she struggled to sit up. "Pops, where are my boys?" she panicked.

"They slept through it all. Take it easy," Freddie replied as he hurried to her side. "Your mother is packing their bags. We are going to watch over them for the weekend."

Detective Shafer informed, "We have a few questions to discuss regarding your sister. It seems that you were the last person who she spoke with."

"Can't this wait till morning?" Freddie asked.

"Come down to the station in the morning," Officer Pease instructed.

Trouble arrived; she interrupted, "Mo!" she screamed. Chassity ran to Monique's side. To her surprise she rushed right past Detective Montavious Shafer, also known to his friends and family as Monte. Chassity felt uneasy about his presence, she now wondered why *he* was really there.

THE TURNING POINT

God does not allow bad things to happen to any of his children. We have a choice to make the best decision, not to benefit us but to benefit the body of the spirit from which we are created. But what about the people who are tied into this arrangement by the people they loved and trusted? Rick loves Monique, he trusts Chassity, and he respects David. Monte is caught in the web of family and friends. Freddie will do anything for his children, except die. Chassity has only one obligation and that is to be loyal. Shelton has a father who is in the penal system and now his mother is dead. Anthony has to maintain a business for his brother at all costs. Orlando loves his step brother but he has to look out for himself. Even Liz, whose role has yet to be revealed, has already played the fool. There is no loyalty, love, respect, or trust. Alex and Ashton have been exposed to the actions of everyone their parents encounter. The truth is seldom exposed before it is too late. We are all guilty of seeking something of the evil…something small….something minor….something we never thought would matter.

DeBAITed Deaths Unknown Face

DAVID

David paced back and forth in his cell. Monique never showed up to visit him. He was worried, she never disobeyed him. When she didn't arrive Saturday, he expected her Sunday. He called all weekend. He normally kept a cool head when it came to Mo. She had a way of getting her point across and standing her ground. He loved that about her, but his ego wouldn't allow anyone to disobey his command. When she didn't show up Saturday morning, he called her cell phone and her home phone several times throughout the day. She never answered, not once. His first thoughts were that she was on the road. Maybe she just simply missed the calls. Visitation hours ended at 3pm. When she didn't answer by 5pm, he feared the worst. Maybe she had an accident. The one person he knew he could call to get her whereabouts was on an assignment. He didn't like his people distracted from their assignments. His thoughts were getting the best of him. Mo has no reason not to answer my calls. She has never missed a call. Something is either up or going down. Which is it? All hell is breaking loose. My time is almost up. What the fuck is really going on? My wife is having an affair with Freddie *and* Monte. Monique's MIA. Damn it! "Tawanna was "KIA" killed in action.

His thoughts shifted. What about Shelton? How is my son? He must be so confused. His heart ached for his son and his son's mother.

He remembered how he met Tawanna. The sisters were in town visiting Chassity that particular weekend. They all partied hard like they always did. Naja had hosted a birthday party at the Pink Poney where she stripped to earn money for law school. That night after a few drinks, Jasmine left early on business. Jasmine trusted Chassity with her sister's well-being.

DeBAITed Deaths Unknown Face

Chassity was into ecstasy and hard liquor in those days. She simply didn't care what happened to Tawanna after her sister left the club. The morning after, Brenda, his girlfriend at the time, woke the neighborhood by honking her car horn in Anthony's driveway. She was on a wild rampage looking for David. Anthony had to instruct Chassity to go outside to make Brenda go away but Brenda would not budge until Chassity agreed to take her to David. She stalled as long as she could by telling Brenda that she hadn't seen "D" since the party at the club. Brenda demanded to know which club. She was disgusted to hear that David would even consider being in the Pink Poney, a popular night club where Caucasian women danced. She drove forty-five minutes to N.E Atlanta looking for her soon to be husband's white Jaguar. Not far from the night club, Brenda spotted the Super 8 Motel. The pit of her stomach began to do flips. She pulled into the parking lot. There it was, parked in plain view. She spotted David's Jag. She ignored Chassity's pleas to let it go. Minutes before check out time, Naja stepped outside from their room to return the key to the office. Brenda gasped as she laid eyes on the 5'11 white woman. Her beautiful red hair flowed down her back. Naja wore a black fitted sundress to compliment her hour glass figure. She walked with confidence, class, and sophistication. In her heart, Brenda realized David's attraction. She knew his taste. Nevertheless, the soon to be Mrs. Brenda Jones-Carter jumped out of her latest model BMW. She followed Naja to the front office. As Naja was leaving the front desk, she turned to see Brenda's slightly tinted complexion, cute freckles and short hair. Brenda, in her years before the scandal, was an image of the actress, Halle Berry. As soon as Brenda caught up to Naja, she met her stance. Brenda demanded to know Naja's identity. She also demanded to know the nature of her affairs with David. Naja noticed her. She just didn't care to waste any of her time explaining anything to her.

DeBAITed Deaths Unknown Face

She simply dismissed Brenda. Naja continued strolling towards his Jaguar that was waiting to pick her up in front of the hotel. Surprised by Brenda's performance, but more so annoyed, David instructed her to lower her voice of accusations. He dared her to continue to publicize his business by causing a scene. Brenda insulted Naja by calling her a cheap trailer trash hooker. That's when Naja vowed to beat the black out of Brenda the next time they met, boasting that she identified the difference in their heritage. During the commotion, the frantic seventeen year old Tawanna was picked up by Monte. Back then, he was one of David's main drivers. She had been waiting in the lobby and watched the entire confrontation. She heard the last of the altercation as she got into the Chevy Caprice. Tawanna wasn't mature enough to understand all that was going on. She got caught up in the alcohol, the party, and the way the crowd accepted her. The attention David had shown her blew her mind. He had even talked her into having a threesome with him and Naja. Regretfully, David knew that was the night Shelton was conceived.

DeBAITed Deaths Unknown Face

BRENDA

Although David had done plenty against Brenda and their covenant, she always felt guilty during and after her affairs. She just wanted David to love her completely. She wanted to feel like the most important being in his life other than God. Her African American mother raised her in a Baptist church. In her lowest feelings of despair, doubt, and heartache, she felt that she needed to lay her burdens at the altar. As she drove her car down Cascade, a small community in South Atlanta, her thoughts of worship lingered. She felt bad. As she drove she prayed.

"Lord, please have mercy. I have sinned against my marriage. I do not love all of my neighbors. I hate my enemies. My love is in money and materials. I know I am not all that I can be or all that I should be. I am just only how I know to be. Lord I am asking you for instruction. Show me how to forgive."

After she parked her Beamer, she retouched her makeup before stepping out into the small parking lot wearing a lavender two piece skirt suit complimented by a silk ivory blouse and ivory shoes all designed by BeBe. Her diamond watch, wedding ring, heart shaped pendant, and matching earrings complimented her attire. David enjoyed spoiling her. She was always beautiful. Once inside the church foyer, she felt uneasy and thought about leaving. Just as she turned to walk towards the exit, a greeter from the church opened the door on the left side of the two way entrance and she made eye contact with Brenda. The greeter offered a warm smile. Behind the make-up of her outward appearance, Brenda's hidden eyes watered behind the dark tint of the shades she wore. She took slow steps down the aisle. She chose a seat on the right side of the church. She continued to fight her tears as the choir sang the southern, soulful rendition of the gospel hymn, "Speak to Me."

DeBAITed Deaths Unknown Face

The pastor who Brenda had not seen in over two years took his stance at the pulpit. His words were profound. The strong words touched her personally as his microphone expanded his words: "The outward appearance is nothing without the right heart on the inside."

The revelation captivated the congregation. They applauded, many shouted, "Amen!" Some stood to their feet, they cried, "Glory!" Others fanned away the humidity in the hot church. The sermon was heartfelt as the pastor preached about restoration, change, focus, obedience, and love. There was a word for Brenda this Sunday that would change a small portion of her spirit. During fellowship after service, the pastor's wife approached her.

"Hello," greeted the pastor's wife with a heartfelt smile coupled with an expression of concern.

"Hi," Brenda responded as she offered a receptive hug of love.

"I know that you do not visit often so I want to take an opportunity to tell you that if you give it to God, he will fix it. There is no need to say a word because it is written all over your face. Know that if I can help you I will. I love you Sister Carter. You are always welcomed."

She cried. All she could manage to say was, "Thank you."

In her car, the words I love you lingered in her ears. No one had told her those words in a very long time. More importantly she had forgotten what those words meant. At that point, she realized just how lonely she truly was. As she cried, tears flowed because of the intense pain she felt as she thought of her marriage, her husband, and herself. The thought of letting go burned her heart. She began to believe that maybe they were never meant to be or that she has just passed through life by a mishap. She dwelled over the memories.

DeBAITed Deaths Unknown Face

In her sorrows she searched to feel real again. She wanted to remember the last time she felt alive. She yearned to feel happiness again.

Her mother had been a prostitute in her youth. Her white father had been a faithful customer to her mother. Once Brenda was born, her grandmother was awarded custody to raise her. Her grandmother died when she was nineteen years old and Brenda inherited $250,000 plus some land. Her estranged father had a college fund set aside for her. Her passion became to help young people with similar obstacles as her own. She achieved a Masters from Ohio State in business and expanded her rental properties throughout the state. By the time she was thirty years old her net worth was close to a million dollars.

She and David met at one of his night clubs. He owned several businesses through his family's connections. He was attracted to her mind more than anything else. He saw a greater investment 'through her', larger than what he really saw 'in her.' Brenda didn't mind. She always tolerated the things that she didn't like about David, like his wandering eyes, the depth of his secrets, his personal turmoil or grief. David never let anyone inside of his heart. She never felt the warmth of his heart, so she settled for the love of his company. The pair grew wealthier through each other. They made enough money to pay for their pain. They had the faces of happiness, the style of confidence. But deep down the pair were two loose cannons. Now in the prime of their lives, under the commitment of God, they were married, living separate, private lives.

Once home, she thought she would be able to relax. She got ready for an evening bath. Her tears dripping in the cool water of her bathtub. She fell into a quiet place and began to moan. Her heart was heavy. Her grandmother had taught her to just moan in her despair. "Pray until you feel better", said the sweet voice of her beloved grandmother.

DeBAITed Deaths Unknown Face

Brenda began to pray. *"Deliver me from evil oh Lord and take this pain away. I surrender oh Lord. I belong to you and I am asking for you. I have been foolish in my ways. Please take me in your arms, Oh gentle Savior please turn it all around. Order my steps and touch my heart. I welcome your spirit over me. Forgive me Lord. Please take over in the name of your son Jesus. I pray that your will is done. Amen"*

She fell silent, still crying. Time passed and not remembering the order of her steps, somehow, someway morning arrived. It was 11 AM. She was awakened by the sun rays shining through the sheer curtains. She sank deeper in her comforter and for the first time in years she said out loud into the atmosphere, "Thank you Lord for this day." She smiled. She was happy to see a new day. She raised her head, stood to her feet, and claimed victory over her future. As she headed down stairs her cordless phone rang.

Without thinking or rehearsing she simply said, "Hello?" then she heard "Press 5 now". She did.

David spoke, "Wassup?"

"Hey, I just got up to make coffee."

"Brenda, Tawanna was killed and I need to know how Shelton is doing."

"Okay," she replied.

"And..." David hesitated. He hated to ask. He expected her to carry on and run with this one.

"Hello?" Brenda encouraged.

"I need to know what is going on with my case."

She couldn't believe that he thought she would call Naja for him. She remained calm. "Doesn't your lawyer take care of that for you?" she responded with a slight chill in her voice.

"She did," he sighed.

She heard his voice crack. Was that panic she thought she heard?

DeBAITed Deaths Unknown Face

"Yea B my lawyer does, but... I need another lawyer now."

He called her "B" as if she was a friend. She felt uneasy. She sat on the steps of their wrap around stairwell. "David, what is wrong?"

He barely murmured, "She's dead B."

"*Dead*," she stated. "Who David?"

He was desperate. He needed his wife. He needed to know what was happening. David was scared for his family. He could not pinpoint what was going on.

"I don't know what happened. All I know is someone shot her. They think she was robbed on the side of the road. I just know that Naja was killed. I'm almost home "B". My son is out there alone, my lawyer is dead, and I can't do anything in here."

He paused as he grew more frustrated. David was dealing with his pain, his confusion, Monique's absence, Brenda's affairs and his personal guilt.

Although she meant well, her words came out wrong. She sounded as if she couldn't care less. "Oh, I didn't know. I will find about Shelton. I guess I will try to see what anyone knows about her."

He couldn't take it. He lost it. "Naja!" Her name is Naja! Find out about Shelton. Find out about Naja, find enough time to stop fucking the country and find enough damn time to be a wife!" He let it all out. He knew.

'Oh God, how did he know?' she wondered. She grabbed her heart. She was speechless. She cried silently. Whispering into the phone, she asked, "David, what do you mean?" He slammed down the phone.

DeBAITed Deaths Unknown Face

Brenda wailed out all of her agony. After a while, she felt peace. She now knew that he knew. She didn't know what he knew, but it brought her comfort to know that he knew something. She no longer had a secret, no longer felt guilty. Now she finally felt hope. She was hopeful that he needed her. She hoped that they could forgive each other. She was hopeful that she could be Shelton's mother. She hoped that she could hire a new lawyer. She wanted to be the one to save her husband. She was hopeful that she had a chance. Her affairs did not bother her anymore. She was hopeful that when the time came to explain, that she would be able to admit her faults. She planned to remind David that she had accepted his indiscretions, so he should accept hers. As she sat in silence, she debated with herself over her feelings toward Naja. After all the years of having to deal with the relationship Naja had with her husband, whether it was business as David had always insisted, or pleasure as Naja always harassed, it no longer mattered. She felt guilty for feeling relief. Relieved that she now had the opportunity to be close to her husband in the way Naja once was. She was now able to be what Tawanna once was. She looked up into the atmosphere as she spoke. "God I don't know what you are doing, but please take my hand."

After brunch at home, she decided to head downtown to the shelter. She arrived around 2 PM. Although it was a typical Monday afternoon for most, she felt like it was a Friday night. She stepped out of her Beamer wearing a two piece black pants suit with thin white pin stripes, black pumps and pearls to compliment it all. She had grabbed her briefcase from the trunk when she turned to face Chassity.

"Where the hell have you been?" Chassity demanded.

Brenda closed her trunk. "Well, good afternoon to you too," she replied.

Chassity was worried. "I have been calling you all morning!"

DeBAITed Deaths Unknown Face

Brenda realized that she had her cell turned off. She reached into her armrest, grabbed her cell phone then powered it on in front of Chassity. The phone buzzed almost three minutes. She had missed text messages and there were several voicemail indications. Looking at Chassity's aggravated expression, she said, "Girl, I am so sorry my mind has been elsewhere. What is going on?"

"What is going on is that Naja is dead and Tawanna's funeral is tomorrow. Everything is driving me crazy. I want out!" Chassity yelled.

Brenda remained calm. She hurt for Chassity; however, she wasn't responsible for her position. "I just heard about Naja from David. What are the details?"

Chassity played mind games. "She is his damn lawyer. He doesn't know what happened?"

Brenda didn't appreciate Chassity's tone. She removed her dark shades and took a step closer. Chassity backed up. Brenda spoke sharply, "He is still in prison. No one is obligated to give him those details, but you ran the streets with her. Therefore, I am asking you what happened to your people Chassity."

Chassity glared at Brenda during her entire response. "All I know is she was stranded by the state line and someone shot her in the head. It looks like she was robbed. No prints or suspects right now. Whoever did it took her cell phone. It's under investigation."

Brenda glared clear into Chassity's eyes. "I can't believe this is happening. I am sorry for your loss. If there is anything that I can do, I will. Who is investigating this for her family?"

Chassity's eyes flinched. Brenda could be so cold. She raised an eyebrow. "Detective Shafer," Chassity answered. "Oh, Monte is a dear friend. He will take care of you," Brenda replied.

DeBAITed Deaths Unknown Face

MONIQUE

Monique had a serious headache driving from the police station. She just could not fathom that Naja was dead. She couldn't wrap her head around her thoughts. Her entire world seemed to be spinning out of control. Officer Pease and Detective Shafer had questioned her for general information. Officer Pease had asked her to tell them about the last time she spoke with her sister, Naja James. They wanted to know the nature of the call, the nature of their relationship. They asked her routine questions including if she knew the last details about what she had going on in her life. She was honest and answered what she knew. However, she only knew what Naja had told her. She repeated what she was told. Naja had visited a client. She was with someone named Bradley. She and her sister had a loving relationship and she didn't know anyone who would want her sister dead. She didn't know of any other details going on in Naja's life at the time.

She ran into traffic on the interstate. She decided to call to check on her boys. After a couple of rings her mother answered.

"Hey sweetie, how is my baby today?"

"I am okay mama. I just can't believe she is gone. Where are Alex and Ashton?"

"Oh sweetheart, didn't you get the message?" Her mother became very concerned.

"No mama. I just left the police station. What is wrong?"

"They are fine baby. I just thought that you knew that Rick had stopped by to pick up the boys. He called this morning to express his concerns…"

Mo interrupted, "Why would you think that I knew that mama?"

DeBAITed Deaths Unknown Face

"Well, when he called, he mentioned that Chassity had called to inform him of the incident and that he should have known we were keeping the boys."

Mo was half listening. What is going on she wondered? Her mother was still talking.

"We left you with Chassity last night. I just assumed you had her to make arrangements for you. Is everything okay Monique?" Her mother sensed something was out of place.

"Yes mama, everything is fine. I just forgot that's all. My head is spinning and traffic is at a stand- still. Let me get off here. I need to call Rick. Everything is fine mama. I Love you both. Tell daddy I am okay."

"Okay Baby. We love you too. Let me know when you get home. I want to come over to sit with you."

"That would be nice mama. I'll call you later. Goodbye." Mo had to go.

Her mother felt reassured. "Okay baby, bye-bye." She clicked off the phone, ending the call.

Mo began to mumble to herself out loud, researching the facts. Chassity wasn't even there when I got up. She left a note saying she would be by later and thanks for the cash. Then Mo looked through her wallet. The money she had aside for Chassity was gone. She couldn't remember anything. What happened after mama and them left? Why can't I remember anything? She grabbed her cell again. She called Rick.

He answered. "Hey Mo. Wassup? Are you okay?"

"Yea, I'm good. Where are the boys?"

The next two voices she heard were Alex and Ashton.

"Hey mama," Alex spoke.

"Where are you?" Ashton asked.

"Hey babies!" Mo felt reluctant, realizing that she had been placed on speaker phone in order to be able to hear both boys. It made it easier for the boys to be able to respond to her.

DeBAITed Deaths Unknown Face

"Mommy is just fine. I have some surprises for you two. After y'all are done hanging out with daddy, he will drop you both off at home, okay?"

Yay, a surprise!" Ashton was ecstatic.

"I hope it's a new Wii game?" Alex guessed, sounding just as happy.

"I will see you two later." She kissed the phone. "Mommy loves you both."

"Love you too mommy," each son replied.

The phone beeped. The background silenced. The speaker was deactivated.

"So what's going on Mo?" Rick asked. He knew she trusted him. He knew she would depend on him if she had too. He still loved her. She still loved him, but he had a temper.

"I don't know Rick. Naja is dead. I just spoke with her yesterday. I thought we were going to meet last night. I fell asleep, but she never called. Now I feel so guilty. I just keep thinking that if I had called her none of this would have happened. I would have known that the car had broken down or that she was lost or that she needed me. Oh my God! Rick my sister is dead!" She broke down.

Rick just sat and listened. All the things his ex-wife and mother of his son were telling him he already knew. He sat silent. Silent because he loved Mo. Silent because Jasmine was sitting beside him listening to the conversation. Silent because his son Ashton and his brother Alex were happy to be spending time with him. He was silent because he had to kill Naja. It was his duty; it was his job. She was nothing more than business to him.

After a few minutes, Mo sniffled. She inhaled and let out a deep sigh to regain her composure.

"Rick, I need some time to figure some things out. How long can you watch the boys?"

DeBAITed Deaths Unknown Face

"They can stay the day, but I am leaving to go out of town tonight. Can I drop them off around 8 tonight?"

"Yea, if I'm not home, mama will be there. Thanks Rick."

"It's all good Mo. Just keep your head up. Everything is going to be alright. I got the boys. They are good, no worries. Just handle ya business. Get yourself together, Mo. I'm sorry for your loss."

"Thanks Rick. I'll see y'all tonight."

"Later," Rick replied. He ended the call.

Monique signaled to get out of traffic. Headed to grab a peace of mind. She turned onto Old National Highway and pulled into the Wal-Mart shopping plaza. She entered the store and racked up on all sorts of gifts for the boys. She felt guilty because the boys missed school, because Naja was dead and because she forgot about David. David! She just realized she had never shown up. He must be worried or worst. He may even be suspicious. Mo feared the worst. "OH GOD," she gasped out loud.

"Are you okay ma'am?" The cashier asked as she continued to scan the items at the check-out counter. Mo flashed back to reality

"Yes, I'm fine. Thanks." She paid for the items then rushed to her car. Mo grabbed her cell phone from her purse to make a call. She remembered David had always told her to call Anthony, his right hand man, if she ever had an emergency.

"Wassup? It's been a while," Anthony teased as he answered the phone.

"Hi Ant. Have you heard from D?"

"No, Why? Wassup?"

Mo rambled, "Look, if you talk to him, please ask him to call me as soon as possible."

"Bet," Ant replied. He clicked off his phone.

DeBAITed Deaths Unknown Face

She sat in her car in a state of panic. Oh God, get me out of this. She wondered how David would feel once he learned of her relationship to Naja. Why would he care? What would it matter? She whispered, "Lord have mercy on me. Please fix this."

Moments passed before she decided to call Chassity. "You have reached Chass…."

Voicemail. Mo clicked off her phone. Chassity called right back.

Monique answered. "What the hell is going on?"

"Hold up, chill Mo, what's wrong? Why are you coming at me like that?"

"Because you told Rick to go get my boys, you told my mama that you were staying with me, and you took my damn money from my purse. I haven't heard from you!" Mo yelled into the phone.

"Mo, you tripping. I did stay with you through the night. I told you I was headed out of town. I hadn't even packed last night when I called you back."

"Called me back for what?"

"You told me to call to let you know for sure if I was coming to get the money. When I did, your mother answered the phone and told me what had happened. That's why I rushed over. This morning I told you I had to go. That's when I said that I would tell Rick to get the boys. You have been so out of it Mo. Are you okay?" she asked sounding concerned.

She sighed. Everything was making sense but she still felt confused. She began to worry. "I can't talk right now."

"Call me if you need too," Chassity offered.

"Aye… Mo interrupted. Where are you going?"

"My friend lost her sister. The funeral is tomorrow."

"That's right," she said, relieved that she finally remembered something. "I will be fine. Have a safe trip."

DeBAITed Deaths Unknown Face

While she was driving home, her phone rang. She didn't look before she answered. "Hello?"

"Hello," the female voice replied.

"Who is this?"

"That depends on how you look at it?"

"Who in the hell is this!" Mo demanded.

"I am the other person who knows you are David's mistress. I know that Naja, your sister, is dead. I know that you want David's money. I know that you don't have anybody in this entire world to have your back."

Mo held the phone, searching for a familiarity in the voice. "Who is this?" she demanded again.

"When David calls you, you better come clean. If you don't, I will expose you for being the low down bitch that you really are. Tell him that it's over. Tell him who your sister is. Tell him everything… or else…"

"Or else what" Mo dared.

"Or else you may need a little roadside assistance as well."

The caller clicked off. She glared at her own reflection through her rear view mirror. At first she felt panicked, and then she thought… Brenda! The caller knew enough things but the caller did not know all things. She grinned. She had a new plan in mind. She pulled her skirt down over her M&M tattoo then called her brother Monte, the detective.

DeBAITed Deaths Unknown Face

JASMINE

Jasmine was in her bedroom packing bags for the rest of the week. Tawanna's funeral would be the next afternoon. She had promised her family that she would stay the remainder of the week, but now she was thinking of staying with them longer, especially for her nephew Shelton.

"Rick?" she called out. He entered the room and kissed the back of her neck. The gesture was sweet but it startled her.

"Stop!" she said.

"What's wrong with you?" he asked.

She stopped packing and asked, "What's going on with your baby mama?

He replied as he sat down on the bed beside the half packed suit case. "She had a death in her family."

"Wow, are you serious? Who was it?" she asked as she pushed the suitcase out of the way making room to sit down on the bed beside Rick.

Shit! He thought to himself, realizing Jasmine was not aware of the news of Naja's death. "I didn't get all the details. Someone from her dad's side of the family," he lied.

She sat and stared at Rick. She knew what she had heard through the phone. She urged him to elaborate,

"Does Monique know Naja?"

"Know who?"

"Rick, don't give me that shit."

The phone rang interrupting their budding brawl.

"The phone just saved your ass," he said as he tossed her the cordless. He left the room to go smoke a cigarette on the patio.

Annoyed by the distraction, "Hello?" Jasmine greeted.

"What time are we leaving?" Chassity asked.

"I don't know. Rick has the boys and he told Monique he was dropping them off around eight tonight, so I guess after then."

"Cool, call me after y'all drop them off. Then we…" Jasmine interrupted, "Chassity?"

She paused. Chassity felt the tension through the line.

"What's going on? I asked you about Rick's baby mama before. You never got back to me and now I'm feeling like I'm in the dark on a few details."

"Why do you feel like that?"

Jasmine raised her voice. "Rick was on the phone with Monique earlier and I could have sworn that I heard her mention Naja's name. I asked him about it but now he's stuck on stupid all of a sudden, like I am speaking French. I wanna know what the hell is going on!"

Chassity kept her cool. "Gurl you are tripping. I know Monique but I don't be in her business like that. You know Rick don't tell nobody nothing. Maybe you didn't hear what you thought you heard. Anyway, "O" 'bout to take me home so I can pick up my things. Just call me when it's time to meet up."

She knew better. "Yea I will. Maybe I can get answers from both of y'all at the same time."

She clicked Chassity off her line and called Naja's cell phone. *"The caller you are trying to reach cannot be located."* She tossed the phone across the bed. She didn't think anything of the message. She had heard it before so she assumed Naja was still traveling. She finished packing and then went into the restroom for a quick shower.

As she washed her tangled curly hair, she sobbed over the anticipation of her sister's funeral. She cried harder as she thought of Shelton. Her eyes were closed as she thought of her sister's short life. She had no damn business over there fighting a man's war. None of this would have ever happened if she hadn't fallen for D. I should have never trusted Chassity. I should have cut Brenda off. None of these people matter now. My sister ran to the army to get away from this shit! And now she's *dead!*

DeBAITed Deaths Unknown Face

She fell into the shower and began to scream hysterically. She felt guilty about their past. "I killed my sister!" she screamed. "Oh God! I killed her! I should have never left her with that bitch. I knew Chassity would leave her!"

Rick ran into the bathroom. He grabbed a towel from the rack. Jas had cut her head on the temperature knob.

She just kept screaming and wailing, "I killed my sister. I killed my sister!

He picked her naked, wet body up from the side of the tub and carried her to her bed. She began swinging her arms hitting and kicking him.

"Get away from me!" she screamed. He kept trying to console her.

"GO! Get outta here Rick. Something isn't right. I can't trust you! I hate you. God, I hate everybody!" she screamed hysterically.

Alex began beating outside the locked bedroom door. "Rick! What's wrong? We want to go home." Ashton began to cry, "I'm scared Daddy."

Nothing meant more to Rick than those two little boys. They were the only honest parts of his life. Nobody mattered to him more than Ashton and Alex. He yelled at the door, "I'm coming out Alex. Take Ash outside for me. Everything is okay. Go now!"

He turned and grabbed Jasmine by her neck. He covered her mouth with his right hand as he pressed his forearm into her chest. He looked her dead in her eyes and whispered, "Shut the fuck up! My boys are here and they are scared! I will punch you in your face if you scream again. When I let you go, you get up, you get dressed, and you walk outside. Do you fucking understand me?"

Wide eyed, shocked beyond belief and scared half to death, she nodded. As she lay stiff under Rick's firm body, he pressed her back harder. He released her, got off of her, and then walked out of the room.

DeBAITed Deaths Unknown Face

She was mortified. She had heard stories of Rick's temper, but never experienced the wrath of it. When he got to the front steps outside, Ashton was still crying.

Alex asked, "What's wrong with Ms. Jas?"

Rick stood in front of the boys. "She is fine. Come on, let me take y'all home." He picked both boys up and carried them to the car.

After securing the boys into their safety belts, he stood behind the car to smoke a cigarette while he called Monique. It was earlier than expected so he needed to make sure someone would be there.

Mo answered, "Hello?"

"Hey Mo. Look, I need to bring the boys home now. Is that cool?"

"Yea, bring them now. I am here."

"Cool." He clicked off the phone.

When he looked up, he saw Jasmine locking the door. He walked up the steps and grabbed her bags. Neither of them spoke or looked at each other. Everyone was quiet as they listened to a local hip hop radio. "Be Easy" by Atlanta's artist T.I blared through the speakers of the black Acura.
Rick bobbed his head along with the lyrics as he rapped along. *"Be easy, you don't won't no problems wit' me."* He glanced over at Jasmine. She glared at him, still shocked by his volatile mood swing. Rick acted as if nothing had happened minutes before. When they pulled up in front of Mo's house, the boys bolted through the front yard, running into the house. He jogged to catch up leaving Jas in the car. He rushed to interrupt any explanation of what the boys would tell their mother.

"Hey babies!" Mo greeted as she fell to her knees hugging the boys, kissing them all over their faces. She was so happy to see them, including Rick.

"We were scared Mommy!" Ashton shouted.

DeBAITed Deaths Unknown Face

"Scared?" Mo questioned as she glanced from the boys to Rick.

Rick explained. "Nah, they weren't scared Mo. Jas is going through a little something. She lost it in her room by herself, not in front of the boys."

Monique ignored him. She focused on her boys and their reactions. She specifically asked, "Are you okay Alex and why were you scared Ashton?"

"I just heard screaming," Alex stated.

"I heard her say the word kill," Ashton informed.

Mo yelled, "KILL? Both of you go to your rooms. We will finish talking when your father leaves. Everything is okay now. You're home."

Both boys said bye as they ran off to their rooms. Rick waved goodbye as he accepted the stare Monique was giving him. She began to walk towards Rick, but she saw Jas was standing on her front porch. Jasmine wore a black jogging suit with black Reeboks and dark shades. Her thick wavy pony tail flowed out of the back of her black "A" ball cap. She looked at Jas, then to Rick. She changed her direction and opened the protective door. "Come on in." Monique invited Jasmine.

Jasmine stepped into the foyer and stood. She greeted, "Hey Monique."

"Hey," she replied. "So my children heard the word 'kill' and screaming huh? So what happened at Jasmine's house that would not have happened at your apartment if that is where you would have been with my boys?" Mo demanded.

Jasmine spoke up instead. "It was my fault Monique. I just lost my sister. I was feeling down, aggravated, and guilty. I just…"

"Shut the fuck up!" Rick interrupted. He began walking towards Jasmine.

DeBAITed Deaths Unknown Face

Monique stepped in front of Jasmine. She already knew how it was about to go down. "NOT TODAY! Outside! Outside now! " she yelled over everyone.

Out in the yard, she informed both of them. "This is not how we handle things where my boys lay their heads." Jasmine saw Rick turn red again. She ran across the lawn to the car. Monique was right behind her. Rick watched from the front door. He took time to light a cigarette and then scrolled down the driveway.

"What happened?" Mo demanded. Nobody spoke. Jasmine sat in the passenger seat and dropped her head. Rick continued to smoke as he glared at Monique and waited for any wrong moves. Jasmine looked past Monique to see Rick. He met her eyes as he hawked up saliva and spit across the front yard. Afterwards, he flicked his cigarette butt into the same direction. Rick anticipated Jasmine's answer. Monique knew it. Jasmine knew it too.

"Okay," Mo began. "Look Jasmine, it's like this. I don't really even know you. You seem okay but this is the second time you have been around my children. This is the second time they have had something to say when they got home. I don't think it is a good idea for Rick to have you around the boys. Don't take it personal."

Jasmine was offended. "What? I have been nothing but good to your boys."

"Be that as it may, I still don't want you around them. I don't smoke, period. Now I understand you may be going through something, but since you can't handle yourself better around my children, I would rather that you not be around them at all. Take it how you wanna take it, but that's all I am going to say about it."

"Cool," Jasmine stated.

Rick didn't say a word. He just walked around the front of the car and slid into the driver seat.

"Rick?" Mo called.

DeBAITed Deaths Unknown Face

He looked at her. "What?"

She ignored his attitude. "I needed to speak to you alone about something else."

He ignored her wishes. "We gotta go."

Jasmine interrupted in a light tone, "It's cool. We have time. I already told Chassity that I would call her around eight."

Jasmine waited to see if Monique heard her bait.

Mo interrupted. She poked her head in through the passenger window to stare at Rick. "Chassity? I know it's not the same Chassity we know is it Rick?"

Rick was pissed. "You talk too fucking much!" he yelled as Jasmine cringed in her seat.

Mo wanted to know. "Are you talking about Chassity Waters?"

Rick jumped out of the car, took his cell phone from his back pocket, and began to walk back up the driveway to sit on the steps. He had to talk to Chassity.

Jasmine wanted to know too. "Yes, do you know her?"

Mo was careful. "Chassity and I go way back. Wow it is a small world."

Jasmine made a mental note. "Really? Okay, you're right, this is a very small world."

Mo presented her bait. "I am sorry to hear about your sister."

Game recognized game. "Thanks," Jas replied, as she removed her dark shades.

Jas was sincere but she was also searching for her answer. "I am sorry for your loss too."

Monique knew there was more Jasmine wanted to say so she nudged her. "Death is so unexpected. I never thought I would lose my sister so early in life."

Jasmine shared a picture from her cell phone.

"This is my sister Tawanna. She was one of the recent soldiers killed in Iraq."

DeBAITed Deaths Unknown Face

Monique damn near fainted. She now knew more than Jasmine. She leveled the playing ground.

"She's pretty. My sister was Naja James. She was a defense attorney. Someone killed her the other night."

At that moment, something transpired between Monique and Jasmine. They both knew what they could not say. The ladies made eye contact for the very first time. The people in their lives were the same, yet at that moment for some reason the strangers felt closely drawn to one another. Maybe because of their situation, maybe because of Rick or maybe it was because of Chassity. They both felt for their sisters whom years before shared their bodies with the same man. Jasmine knew she would not be coming back. That would be the last day they ever saw each other.

DeBAITed Deaths Unknown Face

DAVID

David was in line to use the phone. He had been up all night thinking. Today his baby mama would be laid to rest. He needed to know what had happened to his lawyer. He called Anthony.

"Wassup man? I've been waiting on your call."

"Red flat lined man and Mo called yesterday saying she needed to talk to you ASAP."

"Mo called you? Wassup man?

"Loose ends man. I ain't sure where it's going down at."

David interrupted Ant. "Aye man, get with "B" and come get me out of here. I will deal with Mo."

"Bet." Anthony ended the call.

Back in his unit, David felt relieved that Mo was okay, but he was still confused. He began to think as he completed his push-ups. Mo came up missing the same weekend that Naja was found dead. Afterwards, Mo called Anthony. There has to be a connection, but what is it? He felt angered, he felt betrayed. He left his unit to call Mo.

"Hello?" she answered.

"Mo, what's going on?" His tone lightened when he actually heard her voice.

"I can't lie to you "D". There are some things we need to clear up."

He interrupted, "Start with what you know about my lawyer."

"She was my sister." Mo began to cry.

"What did you just say? She was your what? HOW!" David yelled.

"Baby, Freddie raised her. He adopted her. It didn't have anything to do with you. She never discussed you with me. That was a lie, but Mo was trying to save her own ass now.

DeBAITed Deaths Unknown Face

"I never discussed us to her. I didn't come see you because Freddie and the cops showed up the same night I was going to leave. I've just been losing my mind. Baby I am sorry. I am so sorry but you've got to believe me," Mo continued to sob.

David's thoughts shifted. He needed to know more. "What did she tell you about me? How long have you known that your sister was my defense lawyer? You bitches set me up!" Instantly David hated Monique.

Mo heard the disregard for her grief in his voice. She finally realized that all the ammunition she thought she had was nothing. Without Naja, she now doubted everything about everybody. At this point she didn't give a damn about David either. She just wanted to live her life and raise her boys. She gave him the business, screaming until she had spoken her peace,

"I know that Brenda is your wife. David all I ever asked was for you to tell me the truth. For Naja it was more, but I really felt that we would be able to be happy together."

Her words stung his ears and burned his heart. He felt defeated. After a few seconds he broke the intense silence. Her sniffles continued to come through the ear piece, but he checked out emotionally,

"Monique, you know the truth. You have always known the truth. You decided to play me for your own personal gain. You allowed Naja to manipulate me. Hell, you do not even know how deep this goes. You may know of Brenda, but your problem is you don't know about Brenda. Pick your own battles Mo." He held the line, lost in his thoughts.

He knew that Brenda tolerated him because she deserved him. No other woman came as close to taking her place, except Monique. Now, Monique would never really know that. Brenda was capable of many things. David knew her capabilities. That's what he loved about his wife. They were connected.

DeBAITed Deaths Unknown Face

He continued, "I would have left Brenda a long time ago if it was easy. What do you know about Tawanna?" he urged, as he began to put the pieces together in his head. He had to get the details to uncover the story, behind her story.

"Ta..." she began.

"Don't lie to me Monique," he advised.

She told all she knew. She was desperate for forgiveness from David.

"Her sister, Jasmine, is kicking it with Rick. I found out about her today when Jasmine showed me her picture."

She had more questions, her mind was racing too. "David, why didn't you ever tell me about Tawanna or Shelton? Were they lies too David?"

"You could have told me about them too. None of this was a lie. They were just things that I didn't tell you. It wasn't time. With me in prison, nothing would have changed. Brenda, Tawanna, or Shelton, they are all investments into my life."

Determined to drive her away, he wanted to drown her in her pity. She no longer had a purpose in his life.

"You were the only thing that I loved that didn't have any strings attached Mo, but you have played me. You have betrayed me. You knew Brenda was my wife when you sent me the picture of her with your Pops. All this time you have been playing me through your pops, your sister, and... Brenda. What is in it for you Mo?"

His statements and questions stunned her. She was speechless. She predicted where this was going. She barely pushed out her words. "Don't do this David, not now"

Too late, he had already reeled her in. She had already eaten the bait.

DeBAITed Deaths Unknown Face

"You did this Mo," David simply stated. He ended it and then placed the phone onto the receiver. As he walked back to his unit, his brain raced with his heart. He couldn't feel anything. His parole was a week and a half away. Everything in life was unfolding and he didn't have the freedom to fix it. All of his connections on the outside were caving and he couldn't think of anyone who he could trust. He began to think of everyone that had anything to gain or everything to lose. He knew from the news coverage that the hit was professional, which confirmed his thoughts. He recognized Rick's work.

His frustrations grew by the second. He didn't know how much more he could take. Naja had deceived him. He was now glad she was dead. Brenda was cheating, Mo was a manipulator. The only other innocence he knew had already died for a country that would never know her, Tawanna. His thoughts shifted to Jasmine. He replayed the night he was with Naja & Tawanna, and he remembered how Brenda had caught them. He understood the hatred Brenda had for Naja. His thoughts shifted again as he made the connections. Rick & Jasmine, Mo & Rick, Brenda & Freddie, Monique & Naja Brenda & Monte. He was thinking fast. His thoughts shifted to his letters he mailed. Crap! His letters!

"Damn it! Chassity!"

He wondered who Naja had used to distract his daughter. Suddenly he became relieved. He was certain that Chassity's relation to him was unknown.

DeBAITed Deaths Unknown Face

BRENDA

Anthony left another message at the shelter for Brenda. He told her to meet him downtown in Atlanta at the Westin Hotel in the lobby at 6 pm. She stopped by her home to change clothes. She arrived at the hotel five minutes before the hour. She stepped out of her Beamer wearing a white cashmere sweater, fitted dark printed Calvin Klein jeans, and multi colored heels with a matching hand bag, compliments of Gucci. She handed the driver her car keys and took the valet ticket. Once inside she scanned the area not sure what to expect. She wasn't thrilled about seeing Anthony. They had not always seen eye to eye. She did however accept his knowledge of business. She respected him, otherwise she would not have considered meeting with him. She took a seat in the lobby. Seconds later, she looked up to see the tall, tan, slender built Italian. Anthony wore a black Armani suit, shirt, and shoes.

"Wassup B? How ya been?" he greeted.

"All is well Anthony. What is this about?"

""D" needs to get home; he has business to take care of. When he called, he asked me to handle it," Anthony stated as he took a seat on the couch beside her.

"David is an adult. "D" is not his name," Brenda corrected. "Yes, we will need to get him another lawyer. I have one in mind. It's tragic that all of these misfortunes have taken place. The timing is all wrong."

"Who do you have in mind?"

"Bradley Madison."

"Who is that?"

"Bradley and the deceased worked closely together. I just think it's too late in the game to involve anyone else."

"What does "D" think about this?"

DeBAITed Deaths Unknown Face

"He doesn't think about anything other than himself. I am going to take care of his affairs from this point on. Thanks for meeting with me today Anthony. If there is nothing more to discuss, I will be leaving now."

She spoke as she stood. She placed on her dark shades, pausing long enough to glance at Anthony.

He knew she would be difficult and cocky. Instead, he dismissed her. He knew what he had to do,

"Just get him home to his kid B," Anthony replied as he walked past Brenda without looking at her or looking back.

He left the premises. He needed to head to the south side of town to see what was really going on.

Brenda decided to have a drink at the bar before departing. She also wanted to take the time to finish some other business; return some phone calls.

"I will have a Patron with lime please," she ordered as she began to scan through her cell phone.

"You are a busy lady Mrs. Carter." Brenda knew the voice before she saw his face.

"You've been busy as well. Your latest problem has been a thorn in my ass," she replied as she turned the high bar stool half an angle to make eye contact with Monte.

"How so?" he asked.

"The deceased was David's lawyer. Her incident occurred weeks before his release and now I have to figure out what to do about Shelton."

"Who is Shelton?"

"Shelton is his son with Tawanna, the soldier who was killed over-seas. She was laid to rest today."

"Sounds like you are married to quite the character," he chuckled.

"What are you doing here?"

"Actually, I was following you."

She chuckled. "That is funny and why would you be following me?"

DeBAITed Deaths Unknown Face

Officer Pease approached Detective Shafer and Brenda Jones Carter. "Mrs. Carter, we have questions to ask you about the homicide of Naja James. Come with us quietly down to the office please," Officer Pease informed.

"What in the hell is this about Monte?" she demanded.

"Let's go," Detective Shafer ordered as he patted Officer Pease on the shoulder while walking past him.

They escorted her down the steps in front of the hotel and placed her into a black unmarked Crown Victoria with tinted windows.

"I will sue this entire city for every pothole it is worth. How dare you! How dare you!" she screamed from the back seat.

"Calm down Mrs. Carter. We only want to question you," advised Officer Pease.

Detective Monte Shafer drove quietly. He pulled into the back of the Police Department, parked, and escorted her into the interrogation room. Her light complexion held a pinkish tint. She was furious. She was more humiliated than anything.

"What in the hell could I possibly know about this shit?" she screamed.

"You are not under arrest Mrs. Carter. We are only trying to figure out who would have wanted Ms. James dead. Who may have had a motive? We're talking to anyone with any information. Cooperate and you will be free to go, otherwise, call a lawyer!" shouted Detective Shafer, as he glared into her eyes. He glared at her as he sucked his teeth.

She wanted to kill him. What was he doing? She thought.

"Are you trying to frame me?" she asked coldly. She glared into Monte's eyes.

"Help you," Monte simply stated. "Now let's get started." He always wanted her attention. Now he had it. "How do you know Naja James?"

"She was my husband's defense lawyer."

DeBAITed Deaths Unknown Face

"Did they have an affair prior to his arrest?"
"Yes."
"You referred to Ms. James as my latest problem earlier in the lobby. Please elaborate Mrs. Carter."

Did he really think she would fold under pressure? She saw fire before she spat it out. "Do you really wanna go there with me Monte?" she dared.

He dared her back. "Understand ONE thing Mrs. Carter. My jurisdiction is Glynn County. My personal affairs are in Atlanta. We have a dead body in MY jurisdiction. Her affiliations with YOUR husband are critical. If you want to make this personal be my guest, but remember, I am your only hope!" He was on a roll. "Now you have motive, means, and opportunity. Do you want to cooperate or do you want a lawyer!"

He slammed his fist on the table and left the room leaving Brenda alone to think. She began to panic, thinking to herself, Oh God, No! Please God! This is not happening! She whispered the Lord's Prayer. The only person she could think to call who would help her was Freddie.

Detective Montavious Shafer returned to the room. "Have you decided Mrs. Carter?"

"I need to make a phone call."

"Right this way," Monte said as he guided her across the hall into a separate office to use the phone.

"Hello," Freddie answered.

"Hey Freddie babe, it's Brenda. I'm in trouble and I need you to help me."

She heard his background silence, before he began to whisper. "Where are you sweetie? And what kind of trouble?"

"I'm at the police station downtown. Please come, I'm scared."

"My wife is leaving out now. I'm on my way. Just hang in there baby."

DeBAITed Deaths Unknown Face

"Oh Freddie, please hurry. Tell them I'm in the interrogation room."

"Okay," he whispered ending the call.

Detective Shafer escorted her back into the interrogation room. "Was that your lawyer?" he asked.

"No, but it was someone who will help me," she answered.

He figured she called Freddie. "I see," Detective Shafer responded.

He proceeded with his questioning. "Where were you last Thursday night Mrs. Carter?"

"After work I visited a friend. I was there most of the evening. I left late that night."

"What is the name of the friend you were visiting?"

"Jasmine Neely."

"What was the nature of that visit?"

"Her sister was killed over-seas. I was offering my condolences."

"Was her sister Private Neely?"

"Yes."

"Mrs. Carter, was Naja James there that evening?" she had had enough!

"Yes! Cut your shit Monte. You were there too. We were all there, Naja, Rick, Jasmine, and Chassity. Half of the city was there. Anybody could have set her up. I hated that bitch, that is no secret, but I wouldn't waste my time having her killed. I had no reason to!" She intentionally said too much.

"No one said anything about anyone being set-up Mrs. Carter," Monte stated for the record. He felt uncomfortable. This was enough. He had pushed her too far.

She used her advantage. "I am done talking. Either arrest me or let me go!"

"This is an investigation Mrs. Carter. You are not to leave the city until we clear you, is that understood?" advised Detective Shafer.

DeBAITed Deaths Unknown Face

She nodded and stormed out of the interrogation room. She went into the restroom, sat on the open toilet, sobbed into her lap. She felt betrayed. It was bad enough that everyone knew how bad she hated Naja, but now she was being interrogated by Monte. She felt like she was walking into fire. She knew their affair was about to be exposed. She became delusional as she thought *'those bitches are haunting me, and David's a curse from hell.'* He is the reason for all of this. She sobbed. She began screaming out loud "GOD WHY WON'T YOU LISTEN TO ME!"

A female officer knocked on the stall. "Is everything okay in there?" the officer asked.

"I'm fine," she answered. She was really on the verge of a breakdown.

Brenda was beside herself. Convicted by her actions, she heaved as she struggled to regain composure. She thought to herself *'If only Freddie and I weren't married.'* In the midst of her emotions that thought seemed to be the only logical peace of mind she had. Back in the day, she and Freddie met at the shelter she owned. She had just put the property on the market. He wanted the property immediately to expand his car lot chain in Atlanta. She had met with him and his lawyer Bradley. Within a couple of hours the paperwork work was completed and the deal was sealed. Freddie admired Brenda's mind of business, her professional meekness, and attentiveness to details. She turned him on. She was everything that he had heard her to be. It was no secret that Brenda had become one of the wealthiest women in the city. Shamefully, her reputation had suffered lacerations due to her husband's discredit. After Freddie closed on the property, he invited Brenda to dinner for a celebrative toast. At first she hesitated, but earlier that same day David had confirmed that he had decided to keep Naja employed as his lawyer, spite their love affair. Brenda decided against her gut feeling. She took Freddie up on his offers, and never told him no.

DeBAITed Deaths Unknown Face

Now, after a few more minutes alone in the stall, she realized that Freddie would be there to pick her up. She felt confident again. She just knew that he would support her and hug her. He was her hope. If all else failed with David, she would be with Freddie. She had no idea that she would meet Monte's dad at the same time that she would meet Freddie's son. As far as she was concerned, Monte would never so much as see her bra strap from inside her shirt again. Monte was a mistake anyway, a drunken fling she thought. She washed her face and patted it dry. She admired her blonde highlights. She dazzled her hands through her curls. She wouldn't dare leave before touching up her eye liner and lip gloss. Right before she walked out of the door she sprayed a nice fragrance over her body, grabbed her shades then headed to the exit. Once she stepped into the hall, she hesitated to consider her sense of direction in the busy precinct. She was guided to walk towards the left once she noticed the exit sign. She continued to follow the signs and they eventually led her to the front counter. At the end of the counter she saw
Freddie talking to someone but she couldn't see who he was talking to over all the people who were passing by. Her view was blocked. She made her way through the crowded lobby. Freddie greeted her with a big hug, she rocked from side to side feeling safe and secure in his arms.

The familiar voice yelled, "Pops!" Detective Montavious Shafer jogged up to the couple as they departed from each other's arm.

"Monte, man I was just headed out. I found my lady friend."

"Mrs. Carter?" Monte questioned. Monte couldn't resist scanning Brenda's face for her reaction. She hid behind her big dark shades but he knew she was mortified.

Freddie was proud. "Yes son. She called me to come here to pick her up. This is the young tender I told you I was looking for in here."

DeBAITed Deaths Unknown Face

Monte smirked and winked at Brenda. "Not bad Pops, not bad at all," he replied.

She thought she would die.

The two men shared a hearty laugh. She looked them over from one to the other. Were they laughing at her? *Oh God no!* she thought.

"Well Freddie if you are done with your reunion, I am ready to leave," she instructed.

"Yes baby, let's get you home so that you can tell me what this is all about."

"I will leave you two be," Monte said as he walked off.

Freddie yelled out, "Oh Monte I almost forgot. Call and check on your sister. She wasn't doing so well last I checked."

"Will do Pop!" Monte yelled back as he waved.

Brenda wanted to collapse. "Take me home Freddie. I am just about to go crazy. I can't stand being in this damn building one more second!"

Inside of Freddie's white, tan leather two seated convertible Mercedes, he drove in silence. Brenda stared out of the window. She started out twisting her fingers nervously. Freddie rubbed her hand softly, squeezing gently to gain her attention.

"What kind of trouble are you in Brenda?"

She was glad he asked. "I don't know Freddie. Someone is dead and they think I may know something about it."

He was puzzled. "How would you know anything like that?"

She explained. "The lady was my husband's defense lawyer. He once had an affair with her before his arrest."

Freddie pulled his hand away to let it hang from his window. He had begun sweating. "Who is the young lady Brenda? What is her name?"

DeBAITed Deaths Unknown Face

She sighed. She seldom called her by her name. She figured that he wouldn't know the deceased anyway so she told him.

"Naja James," she answered.

He almost had a heart attack. Dear Lord. He swerved from the road, he panicked.

"Damn it Freddie! What's wrong with you?" she asked.

Unfortunately his guilt was by association. He blurted it out. "Naja James was my daughter."

She grabbed her heart. "WHAT FREDDIE!!!" No! This is not true. WHAT!"

He scrambled for the right words. "Honey I am just as surprised as you are. Let's calm down, let's put the pieces together."

They sat quietly on side of the road in the median. Her thoughts were becoming overbearing. She was exasperated. "How could it be that Monte is your son Freddie? Now you are telling me that Naja was your daughter? How could this be?"

His thoughts traveled. What kind of mess had he gotten himself into? I'd better just let Monte & Monique handle everything. This isn't part of the bargain. I care about her but my family comes first.

Finally she broke the silence, still clinching her chest. "Freddie, Naja was white. How could she be your daughter? I thought that I met your daughter at the hotdog shop and she was black."

He knew they were over. She knew it too. He wanted her to understand. He was sincere, "Yes, that's right, you met Monique. I call her 'Tootsie'. Naja was adopted when she was a baby. Her race has never been an issue. I loved and raised her as my own."

She moved past that. "What about Monte?"

DeBAITed Deaths Unknown Face

He remained calm. "Monte is my other son from a previous relationship. He and Monique, the one you met, are two weeks apart."

Her mouth hung open. He began to feel uncomfortable. She was disgusted as she repeated Monte's comment against David to confront Freddie. "It sounds like your wife married quite a character. And you never told me any of this Freddie. Why?"

He didn't appreciate her judgments. "At my age the past is where you learn to leave hard times. It's all life Brenda and it's up to you to live it or live up to it."

She heard him loud and clear. "Freddie, I do not like this. I need to come clean with you."

He had an idea of what she was about to confess. "What is it dear?"

She confessed. "Freddie today wasn't my first time meeting Monte. What I am telling you is that today wasn't my first time seeing him but I didn't know that he was your son."

He didn't respond. He just clicked his signal light and merged back into traffic towards the Westin Hotel for her to pick up her car. They rode in silence. Brenda wore teary eyes, a heavy heart, and a guilty conscience. He pulled up to the hotel's valet. He turned to her, feeling bad for many reasons. His nature was to comfort her, but his position was to be loyal to his family. He took one last look at her as he spoke.

"Everything is okay. I know that you didn't kill my daughter… and…. and everything else will work itself out. I have to take care of my family and I can't risk "us" being exposed. Neither one of us can handle that right now. If the time is ever right, I will contact you."

He kissed her cheek as he rubbed a running tear from her eye. "Goodbye," he whispered.

Her heart broke.

DeBAITed Deaths Unknown Face

"Goodbye," she managed to respond. Their affair had finally ended.

She stepped out of his car and she walked away. She never looked back at him as he left. She waited to hand her ticket to the attendant. As she waited for her car, her cell rang. Damn, not David, not now, she thought. Relieved she answered.

"Hello?"

"What's wrong with you?" Chassity asked.

"I'm good but why is your number restricted?"

"I blocked it because I had to borrow a phone. My cell died."

Brenda got into her car. As she headed home she continued the conversation. She wanted to be alone. "What do you need Chassity? I have a lot on my plate. I just want to get home."

"I need a ride from the bus station."

"Why? Where are you?"

Chassity reminded her. "I came down with Jasmine for Tawanna's funeral. She is staying but I gotta get back." Brenda put her own heartache aside. She felt great compassion for her stepson. "Poor baby, how is Shelton Chassity?"

Chassity didn't want to get into that. "They told him that his mom is an angel. Nobody is sad around him. He seems so happy that she is an angel. The funeral was difficult. Shelton was very brave."

She was speechless. Tears flowed from her eyes. She finally spoke. "Call me when your bus arrives."

"Okay," Chassity replied ending the call.

The rain caused traffic to pile up. She began thinking, it seems like the more I pray, the more things turn upside down. I can't believe I am in the middle of a murder mystery. None of this was supposed to happen. I wonder who killed her *and* why would they suspect me? The only person who

DeBAITed Deaths Unknown Face

I can trust is David. She began to bargain with herself. I can't afford to lose the half that I have earned and I can't afford to battle this alone. God, please answer my prayer. I've confessed my sins to you. Help me right my wrong. Whatever it is that I have to do to get my life back I will do. Please present the opportunity… Jesus, Jesus, Jesus."

Her phone rang again. The name Anthony flashed on her cell. She answered, "Yes?"

"Meet me at the food court inside the mall in Union City," he ordered.

His voice irritated her. "That is twenty minutes out of my way. For what?"

"I have more info about "D," he stated.

"Anthony, what are you talking about? What kind of information about David?"

"Twenty minutes, be there." He ended the call.

She powered her phone off. She was so tired of bad news, her body felt numb. She swerved in and out of traffic as she battled the rain. Although she did not want to see him, she hated being late. The closer she got, the heavier her anticipation grew, the harder her heart pounded. She arrived five minutes late. As she walked in, he met her midway. Orlando was with him. He met Brenda a few times before with Chassity. His clean cut appearance held Brenda's favor, but not her attention. Orlando was 5'11 medium muscular build, dark goatee, dark eyes and a smooth bald head. He wore black business pants, a crisp white tailored shirt, and black Stacy Adams. She approached them silently. Orlando spoke first.

"Hello Mrs. Carter."

"Hello Orlando," she replied. "What is this about?"

Anthony led them to a secluded table for privacy. "Let's sit over here," he said.

DeBAITed Deaths Unknown Face

Brenda grew agitated. "Someone please tell me something."

"You are in danger," Anthony responded.

"How?"

"Word is that you have been set up in Naja's murder."

"How did you get this information?"

Anthony tilted his head to stare into her eyes. The transmission of the stare reminded her that Anthony was well connected, regardless of how she felt about his presence. He too was a business man. She knew he had information. Nevertheless, she would never jeopardize her character.

"I thought you said this meeting was about David?" she reminded.

"It is."

"How so? Get to the point."

Anthony told her flat out. "This is about David's money."

That was funny to her. "HA! David's what? David has investments, hell even I'm an investment to him. I liquidated our assets. He was just an investor."

"Exactly," Anthony replied, "and if you are dead or in jail then he gets the money. He will be home next Friday."

Whoa! Major news flash to her. "Next Friday! How?"

"Lower your voice," he advised.

She insisted, "What is going on Anthony? Spit it out. Tell me what you know."

Meanwhile, Orlando walked around the general location but remained in ear shot.

"Do you know Monique?" he asked.

She thought about her answer. "Monique? No....I...Wait a minute. Yes, she's David's latest discrepancy," she replied.

Anthony leaned towards her as he pulled his wallet from his jacket. He pulled the picture from his wallet. He watched her closely as he pushed the picture across to her.

"Who is this guy?" Anthony asked as he pointed to Freddie in the picture.

DeBAITed Deaths Unknown Face

She stared at the picture. It was the same picture that Monique mailed to David, the picture they took from the hotdog stand.

She turned pale, everything in her twisted as she looked at herself. There she was in the picture wearing her yellow sundress, with the white, dark yellow and thin black swirls. She stood dead smack in the center between Freddie and Monique. How devastating. She wanted to die. The enemy was kicking her ass. She finally gasped, "That's Freddie and that's Monique! She barely believed her words.

Anthony held his gaze as he broke the news to her. "Yes, Brenda, that is Monique. You've been set up."

She laid her head on the table. She felt as if she would vomit. The room began to spin, her head was pounding and all she could hear or understand were the clear words of "set-up." It all made sense now. The cookout, Monte's advances, Freddie, Monique, and Naja. She had been screwed by their entire family. All of them were connected, they knew it all. They knew it all through Naja. That fact alone felt like a twisting knife in her heart. Not only was Naja dead, she was trying to kill her too. She was losing it. She contemplated if it was possible for Naja to be resurrected through her sister Monique.

She panicked, "Oh God what about David?"

Anthony turned cold. "He knows. He sent me the photo. Monique mailed it to him as part of her scheme, but if you had not been unfaithful none of this would be happening."

She had to hear the words. "He knows what?" she asked.

He boldly told her. "He knows everything that you have done. His parole hearing is next Friday. Expect him to be released. Unfortunately, I have to keep you and him alive until then."

"ALIVE!" she yelled. "Are you serious? No one is going to harm me."

DeBAITed Deaths Unknown Face

He no longer respected her. "Wake up B. Do you think all of this is a coincidence? We all know that Naja didn't kill herself and the Brady Bunch sure as hell didn't either. Someone else knows something."

The entire sitcom was more than she felt she could bear. She rubbed her temples, her head pounded. She tormented herself in her thoughts. *'Oh God, I can't handle this. I knew his whores would cause us to lose everything we have. How could he have been so careless? Damn it! How could I have been so vulnerable?'* She stood up to leave.

"Don't go home," Anthony advised.

"Why not?"

He stepped in front of her. "You gave Monte access to the house and he knows the layout."

The thought sent chills through her body. Her thoughts shifted. "I have to pick Chassity up tonight. What will I tell her?"

Orlando interrupted, "When did she call you?"

"Earlier."

"Where is she?" asked Anthony.

Brenda remained quiet as she stared between the two men.

"She left with Jasmine and Rick for Tawanna's funeral," replied Orlando.

Anthony started barking orders. "When she calls, don't say anything. You pick her up, drop her off, and just keep moving. Do not go home Brenda."

"Okay. When will I know if it's okay to go home?"

"Wait on my call."

They all exited the mall; headed in different directions. As soon as she got inside her car, she locked her doors, fastened her seatbelt, and sped out of the parking lot. At a stop sign she pulled out her cell phone and powered it on. Seconds later she had a text vibration. It read: "I will be at the stop in Union City in 45 minutes."

"Damn it!" She called Chassity's phone.

DeBAITed Deaths Unknown Face

"We are ten minutes away," Chassity answered.
"I didn't expect you until later."
"I didn't tell you that."
Brenda lost focus, she had to ask. She had to know. She was on the edge. "Chassity, do you know Monte's sister, Monique?"

DeBAITed Deaths Unknown Face

MONIQUE

Monique, Alex, and Ashton had fallen asleep from watching a movie when the doorbell rang. She eased up from her bed to look over at the boys. They continued to sleep. She went to see who was at the door. She peeped through the peep hole, unlocked the locks, and opened it.

"Hey Daddy," she greeted.

"Hey Tootsie, "Freddie replied as he walked in past her, taking a seat on the couch. "Arrangements for Naja have been made. She will be cremated per her wishes."

"What about her remains?"

"Well honey her wishes were to be sprinkled over her parents. Those arrangements have been made as well."

"So that's it? She's dead and gone?" She began to weep. "That's it daddy?" She snapped her fingers. "Poof she's gone!" she cried.

Freddie stood to console her. His 5"8 statue met her stance as she swayed back and forth in her father's arms.

"She's in a better place. It is best that things are handled quickly and quietly." He took a step back from her and looked into her teary eyes. "We need to talk about a few other things Monique."

She knew by his tone that he was serious. He never called her by her name unless he was upset with her. "What is it daddy?"

"I saw your brother at the police station today. He had Brenda pulled in for interrogation."

He was annoying her. She wanted to nap with her boys. She didn't want to take the time out for this.

"I am more concerned about you. Did you know that she was seeing your brother?" he asked.

"Yes daddy, I did."

DeBAITed Deaths Unknown Face

"Honey, your sister was executed, not robbed. There is a murder investigation. I had a chance to speak briefly with Monte alone and he told me that he can only scare Brenda for a few days. Now he told me about someone calling your phone. I do not believe that was Brenda. She has more class than that."

She understood and continued to listen,

"Our family has endured a great loss. I allowed you and your sister to put our entire family at risk. My business with this matter is settled. Call your brother. I love you and tell the boys I came to visit." Freddie leaned over and kissed her on her forehead.

"I love you too daddy," she replied just before she heard the front door close. Her father was already on his way. He left the sins they shared on the other side of her door. She stood to walk as she dragged her feet across the floor to lock the front door. Then she moped back across the room and plopped down on the couch. She was determined to get her answers now. The first couple of calls were forwarded to Chassity's voicemail. She hung up each time. The third time Chassity answered.

"Wassup?" Chassity greeted.

"Are you back yet?" Mo asked.

"Yea," her answer lingered.

Monique ignored Chassity's sarcastic tone and went for what she wanted to know.

"Look, I need to know what you know about Brenda. Naja is dead and Freddie just told me that she was questioned. Why haven't you ever told me anything about her? You're supposed to be my friend," she demanded.

Chassity did not appreciate her tone, she became irritated at the fact that Mo was even trying to play her. Now it would be Chassity that determined if Mo would get what she set out to look for.

DeBAITed Deaths Unknown Face

"Hold up! First of all, I stay in my own lane and worry about my own business. NONE of y'all hoes pay me to baby sit so don't come at me like that." She remained cool as a cucumber.

Mo understood. She recognized at that point how well Chassity knew the game.

"Naja is dead Chassity." She let those words linger for a second. "Don't you hear what I am saying?"

Chassity felt for her but she had her own obligations. Business and loyalty was no comparison to what Mo was asking her. She couldn't fold.

"Yea, and I hate that. I just got back from a funeral and I hate that too, but I have to worry about myself."

Mo remained persistent; she went for the punch line. "Was Rick there?" No response. "Was Rick...."

Chassity interrupted. "No. Damn! Quit grilling me. Look, I gotta go." She was annoyed. She ended the call.

Mo slammed the phone down on the base. She wanted to smoke a cigarette but she fought the urge and drank a glass of Merlot instead. She was at odds with herself. Something was up, she felt it. Rick, she thought. She was doubtful that he would tell her anything. It wasn't his style. She knew that her best chance had been with Chassity but she called Rick anyway.

"Yea?" he answered.

"I thought you were out of town with Jasmine for her sister's funeral."

"I didn't go," Rick confided.

She sensed that Rick was feeling down. She knew him well. She thought against using the approach she used with Chassity. "Are you still upset with her about the argument?" Her lightened tone persuaded him to shed some light.

"A lot of shit is happening Mo. Where are the boys?"

"They are napping."

DeBAITed Deaths Unknown Face

He exhaled smoke onto the receiver. "I was on my way over there. You got to lay low for a while."

"Why?"

He realized that she was fishing for information so he bit the bait. "I know Wassup. Monte hit me up earlier. It's too dangerous for my boys right now and it's even more dangerous for you."

Instantly she panicked. "I have a job Rick and all of that is over. Nothing is going to bring her back. It is over Rick," she muttered.

Things were far from over. He knew it, she didn't. He ignored her plea. "I'll be there in a few." He ended the call.

She placed the phone back onto the base. I have got to get myself together. My boys are too young for this. Tears flowed as she prayed.

> "Lord keep me. I trust you. Please forgive me for all the wrong I have done. Please protect us and keep us safe. Keep my children from harm's way. In the name of Jesus. Amen."

She woke up her boys, gave them both a bath, then she began to pack their bags. There would be no sense in trying to change Rick's mind. She knew that he always knew more. She knew that her brother Monte would tell Rick far more than she would know as his sister. Now that Naja was dead, she would have to rely on Monte and Rick. Times like these she regretted cutting all ties with her former friends. Chassity was the only other associate that she had left. Naja had the inside scoop, but now she stood this trial alone. She was standing in her walk in closet when she saw Rick pull in the driveway from the window. He was driving a black Navigator with dark tinted windows. He had cut his hair, now he was bald. He wore dark shades, a black button down shirt, jeans, with black Timberland boots. He looked suspicious. She peeped in the bathroom to tell the boys to finish up, and then she rushed to meet Rick at the door.

DeBAITed Deaths Unknown Face

She felt her nerves bubbling in her guts. She swung the door open whispering loudly, "What is really going on?" she asked him as she stepped outside to stand in front of the door. He was hurting; he was there to handle business. As much as he loved her she was now in harm's way.

"You and Naja went too far," he replied, as he took his shades off and stared into her eyes.

Her voice became shaky, her heart was racing. "What are you talking about Rick," she asked.

He had to tell her. "Listen Mo. The only reason that you are alive…"

"Alive?" She replayed it in her mind. She heard it. He said *alive* as if…how bad could this be? She listened to the rest of his words.

"…Is because you are the mother of my boys. Naja violated my family and that is why she is dead. Now get packed and get in the truck. I'll get the boys." He walked into the house.

In a major hurry, he helped the boys into their jogging suits their mother had left out on their beds. Her voice was low, dare she ask "Where are we going?

"I can't tell you, but y'all will be safe."

"Why can't you tell me?'

He looked at her, he stroked her cheek. The boys were quiet and content as they watched television from the back seat. He felt like he was selling his soul to the devil.

DeBAITed Deaths Unknown Face

JASMINE

Jasmine had her eyes open; she lied still in her childhood bed thinking about all that happened the over the last few days. Their family had witnessed the burial of her sister Tawanna, 'Private Neely,' only twelve hours prior. She cried all the tears she felt that she had. Although she felt alone, she was at peace. She rolled over to face the wall. She could hear her mother humming a spiritual hymn as she prepared breakfast for the family. The house was warm, the atmosphere was full of love and spirit. She missed being home. This was the only place she really felt safe. She wanted to stay and never return back to the city. She had anticipated Rick to be by her side. She couldn't understand why he flipped on her. Before they left to travel, he backed out at the last minute. When she asked him why, he simply stated that she wasn't his speed and that he felt it was best to let her go now, before she got hurt. Those words confused her. She'd replayed them in her head a thousand times on the road. He gave her six hundred dollars, told her to get a rental and to take care of herself. Right before he left he told her to spend time with her family. He kissed her cheek and left her at Enterprise. Chassity had Orlando drop her off. She met Jasmine just as Liz completed the rental for them. From there they got on the road. When she confided to her that Rick ended their relationship, Chassity reminded her that when a man has an honest moment with a woman, he has her best interest at heart. She should only accept the real and move on. Chassity also told her that Rick's heart was still in love with Mo and that everything happened for a reason. Those words hurt her feelings. She had demanded to know why Chassity was being so mean. She wanted to know how she knew so many things, things that she could have told her.

DeBAITed Deaths Unknown Face

Her best friend had taken her hand, looked her in the eyes and reminded her why. Still in bed thinking, her thoughts shifted. Chassity's words were real to her. She had told her...
"Jas I've been in the game a long time, the first rule is never to love with all of your heart, stay in the grey. You and I are different. You expect love from everybody, but the truth is everybody isn't capable of real love. Motives rule the world, not men. Listen to me, we're all grown up now and the game is on another level. The best thing for you to do is to stay focused, live, and help raise Shelton."

She had held Chassity's hand; they shared tears as they traveled on the road. After a few miles down the road, she felt the need to encourage Chassity too.

"When are you going to get out, leave it all behind you?" Chassity didn't answer.

Once they arrived at the crowded home of Jasmine's parents, she ran over to Shelton. He had grown so tall and was very handsome. He inherited his mother's deep dimples and dark curly hair. His stocky body was almost the only trait he had inherited from "D."

"Hi Shelton, auntie's little man!" she cried as she grabbed him and hugged him tight.

"Hi Auntie," he cried and he returned the tight squeeze.

She continued to hold his hand as she weaved through the crowd. She hugged, kissed, and greeted her parents, brothers, close family and other friends.

"How much did you tell him?" she whispered to her mother.

"Awe baby, your father and I just told him that the Lord needed his mother in heaven, that her war on land is over, and that God has called her to be an Angel," her mother whispered and kissed her on the cheek.

DeBAITed Deaths Unknown Face

Jas and Shelton found a quiet place at the picnic table under a large oak tree out in her parent's yard. Meanwhile, Chassity chatted with family and friends. Jasmine inhaled as they sat down, she pressed his head against her chest as she straddled the bench.

"Shelton baby, do you understand what has happened?"

"Yes ma'am, my mommy is gone to heaven. She is dead but she will live in heaven and be an angel forever," he sadly replied.

"How does that make you feel baby?"

"I'm okay Auntie. My daddy sent me a letter. He said that he is going to spend a lot of time with me and he told me that you might stay and live with me if I asked you to." He sounded hopeful.

She held him closer; they sat quietly for a while. She would do anything she could to make his life easier. She and "D" had always just passed one another and they never crossed each other. Her parents didn't care for David and they didn't have the finances to care for Shelton the way he deserved. As she sat rocking Shelton, she made up her mind. She decided that she would meet with "D" once he was home. She decided that she would clean up her act so that she could raise her nephew as her son. She realized that Atlanta was not her home. She noticed Chassity approaching them in the yard.

"Come on baby," Jas whispered as they stood. "Go on in the house and eat Shelton. I will be in after a while."

"How is he Jas?" Chassity asked.

Jasmine dropped her head into her friend's arms. She cried and Chassity held her.

"Everything will work itself out Jas. You know that I will forever have your back. You are the only person outside of my family that I love. It's gonna be okay gurl, just hold on."

"It's going to be a while before I come back Chassity. I may not come back at all. Shelton needs me and I need him."

DeBAITed Deaths Unknown Face

"I understand. I'll be in touch. I have unfinished business in the 'A' but I promise you two will be okay."

She knew that Chassity could keep that promise. They knew everything it was to know about each other. Their friendship was true, a genuine bond. She knew that Chassity would take care of everything. Had the tables been turned the other way, she would have done the same thing for Chassity. The friends knew a lot of things, but they never got in each other's way. They always kept their peace and held their own. She knew that Chassity couldn't just get out or just leave everything in the past. She had chosen the lifestyle that she had adapted to. Chassity was assigned to it. It was a curse that had been inherited. After the memorial service dinner, Chassity packed her bags. She bid her farewell to Shelton and Jasmine's parents. As Jas drove her to the bus station, her thoughts shifted back to the personal rage she felt before the trip. She had to know the answer to the root of the situation.

"Chassity, why did you leave Tawanna alone with David and Naja? What was so important that night that you had to leave? I feel like if you had stayed that...." her comments trailed off.

Chassity was silent as she stared out of the passenger window. She fought back the tears that stung her eyes as she remembered the events of her life that night.

"Jas, do you remember why you left?" Chassity asked. At first she didn't remember. She too had blocked out the events of that night. Jas barely whispered, "I had business the next morning."

Tormented, she recalled the events. "Anthony said it would be okay. Chas, he told me not to worry, he told me that you would understand."

DeBAITed Deaths Unknown Face

"I didn't understand. It was too hard for me to deal with Jas. After you left I partied harder, I blacked out, I let myself go. My only friend was pregnant by my uncle and at the time, I couldn't take care of your sister. I was too worried about you and what would happen if anyone found out."

The night Tawanna was left alone at the club, Shelton was conceived with David and the next morning Jasmine terminated her pregnancy from Anthony. She took Chassity by her hands.

"Let's pray the way we did when we were little. Chassity nodded her head. Jasmine began:

"Oh heavenly Father hallowed be thy name. Your kingdom come, your will be done on earth as it is in heaven. Give us each day our daily bread. Forgive us of our trespasses as we forgive those that have trespass against us..."

Jasmine fell silent. She couldn't finish. Her heart was too heavy to speak. Chassity finished:

"And lead us not into temptation but deliver us from evil. Oh God bless us right now. Please forgive us, watch over us, reunite us, all is well. In the name of Jesus Christ, AMEN

The two hugged. "You gotta bus to catch Shawty," Jasmine teased.

"Girl, you know I got love for you. You sending me back on a bus! A *bus* Jas?" They laughed. "See you later," they said in unison.

Jasmine drove back to her parents. When she arrived, she told her mom, "I'm finally home."

DeBAITed Deaths Unknown Face

BRENDA

"I will have the 7-Pepper sirloin salad please and whatever she is having," Brenda advised the waitress.

"A grey goose with pineapple for me please," Chassity rambled off. Annoyed, she had just hung up on Monique. Now Brenda was breathing down her back demanding answers to questions that she didn't feel obligated to answer. Her attitude was plain as she blurted, "Why the hell are we all the way out here in Camp Creek? Really Brenda, just to have a salad and a drink?" Chassity complained.

Not only did Brenda match her tone, she also clutched her hands together and snarled, "We are here because I picked you up from the bus station and I needed to get away from the city for a while. Listen Chassity, I have known you since you use to pee in the bed and blow spit bubbles! How dare you keep this from me? How long have you known Monique?" she demanded.

Chassity eased back into the booth. All she wanted was to have a drink and go home. She wore a black t-shirt, black jeans, black pumps, a black "A" baseball cap and big silver accessories. She seldom revealed her natural beauty.

"Look Brenda, Mo is no different from the hundred other women from "D's" past. He married YOU. I don't understand why you always expect me to run to tell you every aspect of everybody else's life."

Brenda was silent as the waitress returned to refill her water. She also delivered Chassity's drink. Just as she was about to speak, another server delivered her salad to the table. She pushed it back, her appetite was gone. She was speechless. She sighed as she watched Chassity guzzle down her drink as if it were sweet tea. Her thoughts shifted gears.

"Chassity?"

Chassity looked up at her as she signaled their server to bring her another drink. "Yes," she answered.

DeBAITed Deaths Unknown Face

"Do you think that David ever loved me, only me?" she asked.

Chassity propped one leg up across the booth; she sat up in the corner, finally making eye contact with Brenda,

"I don't know. You should know that. If you didn't know that, then you should not have married him. That's the problem with stuck up women."

Brenda gasped but smiled. Her chuckles came from her teeth. "Explain that one for me," she asked.

"I am not saying that you are stuck up. Don't get me wrong, you are a little bougie. Women like you think that because you have what it takes to pull a particular type of man, that you are better than the rest of us. That's why you compete with every woman he chooses to turn his head to."

"Chassity, I don't compete with anyone."

"Then why are you worried about the rest? All I am saying to you is that you have to be in it to win it if you're going to play the game. If it isn't a game, then you shouldn't be worried."

"This is not a game Chassity. This is a marriage. This is *my* marriage that we are talking about."

"You don't even hear yourself do you?" Chassity asked, as she sat up to receive her fresh drink.

"Am I missing your point?"

"You said this is *your* marriage and that is your problem. You are married to yourself and everything in your marriage has worked for you except David. He goes against everything you want for *your* marriage. You even accepted all of those women. Sure you didn't like it, but you put up with it because you were content being known as his wife. So instead of wondering if he ever really loved you, you should be wondering what *you* really considered love. That's what I think."

DeBAITed Deaths Unknown Face

"You have a lot of advice to be so young. Maybe I should have spent more time growing up and learning the ropes about life before I married anyone," Brenda confided.

"I have a lot to learn too. It's easier for me to tell you what I see than it is for me to avoid making the same choices. That is the reason I believe so many women live in fear of being alone. Maybe we are all messed up in our own way, some worse than others. Who knows?" Chassity added.

"Tell me about Monique. This ordeal with Naja is not going very well. Right now all eyes are on me. I don't care about her and David. That's not important right now. My concern is my freedom. What is she up to?"

Chassity was feeling pretty good. She propped her elbows on the table and rubbed her temples. She giggled to herself and thought...*if you only knew*. She didn't answer Brenda's question, instead she asked, "Hold up, she giggled out loud. Before I tell you anything, I need you to tell me how you ended up freaking Monte and his old ass daddy, Freddie?"

She laughed so hard she slapped the table and rolled back into the booth laughing out loud.

Understanding that she was a little tipsy Brenda laughed with her. The more she thought about the comparison of the men the funnier the scene in her mind became.

"Girl, Monte moves as slow as Freddie. I bet Freddie had it going on twenty years ago," she laughed.

The ladies laughed together. Chassity was cracking up. Suddenly, Brenda stopped laughing. She sat quietly looking at the door. It was Anthony, Orlando, and a bald guy she didn't recognize, Rick. The trio walked over to the table. Anthony pulled a chair from another table and sat at the end of their table. Chassity's laughed trailed into a smile as she acknowledged their company. She kissed her boyfriend Orlando and then nodded her head up at Anthony. Her eyes met Rick; she smiled. "Wassup Slick Rick?"

DeBAITed Deaths Unknown Face

Rick nodded and then turned his eyes to Brenda. He knew her although she had not been acquainted with him.

"What is going on?" Brenda asked.

Rick didn't respond. Anthony spoke first. "Brenda, we need you to leave the city. 'D' is willing to give you a quarter million plus the profit from the sale of the house. He doesn't want you anymore. He wants you to leave or else he will have to get rid of you."

"Damn! Whoa!" Chassity sobered up fast. She sat back.

Brenda stared into Chassity's eyes. She was filled with rage and disappointment. Chassity looked away.

She spoke. "I refuse. If David doesn't want me, he will have to tell me himself." She was trembling all over, but she managed to keep her composure. "What I will do is stay in our home, stay in this city and I will remain in our marriage unless David has the balls to tell me otherwise for himself!"

Anthony, Orlando, and Rick all stood and left. A few minutes passed as the ladies sat in silence. Chassity stood and said, "I'm able to pee now. Shit, I was scared as hell. I thought they were going to kill you in here! I'll be back."

She rushed off to the ladies room.

Brenda was furious. The waitress approached and offered a dessert. "No thanks. Bring me a Patron with lime and the check please."

Moments later, she accepted her drink and in return gave the waitress her credit card.

"Are you okay?" Chassity asked.

"I am fine, but nobody wants me here. I feel like I am losing the battle," she whispered.

The waitress, a small woman with dark hair, wearing eye glasses, returned with Brenda's credit card. She was accompanied by the manger.

"Your card was declined ma'am. Would you like try another method?" the manager asked.

DeBAITed Deaths Unknown Face

Brenda looked at them as if they were at the wrong table. She didn't comprehend what was happening. "Excuse me?" she replied.

The manager responded, "We tried this card twice and it was declined twice. We are happy to try another card or perhaps you would like to pay with cash."

She stared at the waitress and the manager.

"I got it," Chassity announced. She gave them her debit card. The ladies thanked her and left the table.

Brenda could not believe she didn't have the money to cover a forty dollar tab. She sat in the booth silent, feeling defeated and devastated. The waitress returned with Chassity's receipt copy and her debit card. She scribbled her signature and wrote the tip before she stood to leave.

"Lets' go," she stated. She nudged Brenda. "C'mon, lets' go. It ain't that serious, lets' ride."

Brenda dragged herself away from the table. She was lost in her thoughts. They walked through the restaurant to exit the building and all of her thoughts became her reality. She saw her Beamer hooked to a tow truck in the parking lot. Chassity pulled out her cell phone to begin making calls. Brenda began to cry as she whispered, "I've been cut off. Tell me why they are doing this to me."

Chassity was on the phone. "Look, I don't have time for this shit. I'm stranded too, come get me! It's about to rain and I am not walking no motherfucking where!"

The ladies sat inside the foyer of the restaurant on a bench. Brenda laid her head on Chassity's shoulder. Chassity broke the news. "Brenda, I think you should take the offer."

"Why?"

"Look at the situation. Before your affairs you had a lavish lifestyle and half a husband. After your affairs you have no lifestyle and half a husband. Why not settle for a decent lifestyle and no husband? What are you holding on to?"

DeBAITed Deaths Unknown Face

Brenda began to weep. She didn't care that the customers stared as they passed by. She didn't care who saw her. She was sad and she knew Chassity was right but she still couldn't let go.

"I love him," she cried. "I love him so much. Everything I've built I did it for him. I did it for us. Why won't he just forgive me? Oh God what have I done?" she wailed.

Chassity saw head lights flash in the parking lot. "Lets' go," she said.

They walked outside to the black Navigator with dark tinted windows. Chassity hopped in the front, Brenda got in the back passenger side.

"What in the hell were y'all thinking leaving me stuck out here?" Chassity demanded.

Rick was silent. Brenda's cell phone rang. 'Withheld' appeared. Her liver trembled, but she answered. "Hello?"

"Is this Brenda?" the female asked.

"Yes, who's speaking?"

"Hi, I'm Monique, Freddie's daughter. We need to talk."

Rick turned up the radio. He remained silent and ignored Chassity's glare.

"Is that right?" she questioned as she regained her boldness.

"Look, David and I are over. You can have him, his lies, his games, his money, and his bullshit."

Brenda laughed. She silenced her laughter, now serious, "Are you serious bitch? Do you think that you can toy with my life, take me for a joke, use my husband, damage my reputation, destroy my marriage, and leave the fucking pieces behind all because you decided to walk away?"

Monique felt the anger from her voice. It made her uncomfortable; she realized that this woman loved her husband. She felt out of place.

DeBAITed Deaths Unknown Face

"Look Brenda, I understand that I have crossed you. Believe me, it's over. I'm done with all of it. None of it matters to me anymore. I'm sorry."

Brenda sat quietly holding her cell phone to her ear as she stared at Rick's reflection through the rear view mirror. He winked. Brenda grinned.

DeBAITed Deaths Unknown Face

MONIQUE

Monique pressed the "end" button from her brother's cell phone then gave it back to him. Monte took the phone and forwarded the recording between Monique and Brenda to Anthony's cell phone. He then forwarded Rick a copy. She sobbed as she sat on the bathroom floor of a cabin. Rick had locked her inside while her boys were left with Liz. Before he left to meet with Anthony, he made things very clear.
He had told her, "This is business Mo. There was nothing I would not have done for us."
She asked, "Who is that woman with you watching my boys?"
"The boys will be fine."
"I want to talk to Pops. I can't believe you are holding me hostage in this damn bathroom. You're my brother Monte. How could you do this?" she sobbed.
He squatted so that he would be eye level to her. He loved his sister, but he understood the depth of his business with David. At this point, his connection and their lively hood were most important. He looked deep into his sister's eyes; his voice trembled as he spoke.
"Exactly Mo. I am your brother. You allowed me to go behind our father who you knew had been seeing Brenda for three years. You let Naja use me and you did it with her. David isn't some young fool who sells dope for sneaker money. He's connected, he's dangerous, and you have jeopardized our entire family because your scheming ass fell in love with an assumption. How could you trust Naja?
She never gave a damn about any of us. It's daddy's fault for ever bringing that bitch home. I told you that she was shady. I told you not to trust her, just like I told you not to fuck with Rick or Mike, but your problem is that you don't listen! You can't trust nobody Mo! Do you really think that Naja was shot in a robbery, *really?* Well she wasn't.

DeBAITed Deaths Unknown Face

She took 3 shots straight through her right temple! All because she was money hungry and you two dumb asses thought it would work. I am vested in this game. Look around. Can't you see that we all are. The money is *already* in rotation so why would you let Naja trick you into trying to take it all? Think back, how do you think your tuition, medical bills, and first house were paid for? Who do you think keeps my money clean? Where do you think Rick gets his money and cars? How did you think he was able to provide for you? Did you ever ask? Are you seeing this?"
He took a deep breath. "Pay attention to what is going on around you. This world is bigger than you baby girl."

She held her breath the entire time Monte spoke, never taking her eyes off of him. She moved her lips to speak, but no words came out. She tried again. Finally she whispered, but stuttered, "Who-o-o? Mont... Do you know...who killed Na...? Who did it?"

"I can't deal with you right now Mo!"

Those were his last words before he left his sister on the cold bathroom tile. He stood and walked out of the bathroom, locking it from the outside. She cried like a baby new into the world. She was forced to sit on the bathroom floor, her ankles tied together with her wrists in unity behind her back. She had begged them not to cover her mouth in case one of her sons called out for her. She was in disbelief. Monte and Freddie had turned their backs on her. She felt low and she even contemplated suicide, but she couldn't think it through without thinking of her boys. All she knew to do was pray, but she didn't know what to ask for. She felt as if she deserved everything that was happening to her. She believed in God and knew that he was already watching her. She felt as if she was reaping the harvest from the seeds she had sown.

"Mommy?" Alex called.
She kept quiet. "Mommy?" Alex called again.

DeBAITed Deaths Unknown Face

She heard soft knocking on the door by the door knob. She inhaled before she forced herself to speak.

"I hear you baby. I have to finish my hair so that I can run out to the store and get things for our trip. Go make sure Ashton is being good for the nanny and when I get back, I will have a surprise for both of you okay."

Alex pressed his ear against the door and turned the knob. When the knob didn't turn, he gave up. Mo knew Alex was trying to figure out how to get in the bathroom.

"Alex did you hear me baby?"

"Yes ma'am. Mommy, can I see?" he called back.

She then heard the whisper of the nanny telling Alex it was time for dinner.

"I love you Mommy," Alex called out.

She felt very guilty as she forced her words. "I love y'all too."

Her son was no longer at the door. At that moment, she gave in to all the dangers in her mind. She decided to die, she had truly given up. Her body was shaking from her sobs. Her eyes were drenched with tears of hate, anger, lust, greed, and temptation. Mentally, she had checked out. Minutes seemed like days. She felt something moving her. Something was shaking her hard. Now it was shaking her harder. She felt her face burn. She finally began to breathe.

"Are you okay? Baby are you okay?" the voice asked.

She nodded. Rick picked her up from the floor and carried her into the bedroom and laid her flat on her back. She heard him speak to someone. "Stay with her."

Next, she saw Chassity. She was afraid to see Chassity. She began to scream, "Stay away!" as she scurried across the bed. "Stay away from me!" she screamed again! I don't know you! I don't know you!"

Chassity stood still. She watched Mo back herself into the corner.

"Why?" Mo screamed. "Why Chassity?" she demanded.

DeBAITed Deaths Unknown Face

Chassity was aggravated. She moved quickly tossing her weave from her shoulder. She tapped her teeth across her lip ring as she stared at Monique. Chassity finally spoke.

"Why what Mo?"

She couldn't remember. She didn't know exactly what Chassity had done.

"WHY WHAT MO?" Chassity yelled.

"Why is this happening?" Mo cried out.

Chassity laughed. "You did this Mo, I just watched. You better be quiet before you piss them off. Let's talk," she offered.

"I don't trust you," Mo whispered.

Mo was hesitating. She moved slowly to sit on the bed. She shifted back against the headboard. Chassity took four swift steps and pulled a 9mm handgun from her back pocket and pressed it against Monique's head. Her breath was cold, her eyes were grey, and her voice was deep. She meant business. Her tone was harsh and firm.

"I'm supposed to shoot you in your fucking head, then have your boys dropped off at your parents and never look back. Your options are to leave or die!"

Mo whispered, "Where are my boys?"

Chassity held her gaze. The 9 still aimed at Mo's head.

"Please don't do this in front of my boys. Why does this matter to you?" Mo tried to reason. Chassity didn't budge. "Who are you Chassity? Why does this matter to you?" Mo kept talking.

Their eyes met. Chassity's heart raced. She didn't want to kill Mo but if her duty required her to, she would. She wanted Mo to accept the bargain, take her boys and leave… live. She was trained to kill, but she had never killed anyone she loved. She loved Mo because of their history, her advice, their adventures, but her loyalty wasn't with Monique. She was invested much deeper and this moment was about respect, loyalty, and obligation.

DeBAITed Deaths Unknown Face

"Shut the fuck up! Do it or die! Final answer," Chassity demanded. A tear ran down Monique's eye.

"I'll do it," she answered.

She stared at Chassity. Mo's stare turned cold, her lips twisted, and she cocked her head to the side. Her fear was gone. She grew bitter, angered. Not like this, she thought. She snapped. "UGH!" she screamed as she kicked Chassity in the chest.

Chassity gasped! Mo tried to grab Chassity's gun. They struggled over the weapon and the gun fired into the ceiling. Rick and Anthony ran into the room. Anthony grabbed Mo, she was closest to the door. Rick reached for the gun. It fell on the floor and Mo struggled to reach for it. Anthony grabbed the gun first. Mo kicked and clawed, she swung; she fought like a woman in rage. Mo got the gun. She fired the gun again. She aimed it in the direction of the struggle. The gun fired once more. Chassity was shot.

"CHASSITY!" Anthony yelled.

He slapped Mo across the face. She fell to the floor. Rick was already headed out the door with Chassity.

Anthony grabbed Mo by the head and dragged her down the hall like she was a rag doll. "You better pray she lives!" he demanded, as he kicked Mo in her ribs.

Chassity was hit in the shoulder and grazed on her ear. Rick drove quickly as he dialed numbers from his cell phone. Mo was taped down in the back seat on the floor next to Anthony. Swerving in and out of traffic, Rick lit a cigarette.

"I'm about 5 miles out. Meet us there," Rick said to the person on the phone.

"Dr. Michaels, now please." he said quickly. He smoked as he waited, focused on the road. He passed more cars as he continued to dodge traffic.

"Yea, it's me! We had an incident tonight, cover me. I'll be in emergency in 5 minutes." He ended the call.

DeBAITed Deaths Unknown Face

Chassity moaned and cursed, she cried out in pain. Rick didn't touch her. He didn't look at her. Anthony held her hand.

"Hang in there kid, you're gonna make it," Anthony said. He looked down at Mo. She looked up at him, no tears in her eyes.

Anthony hated Monique. "You worthless bitch."

"ENOUGH!" Rick yelled. His eyes met Anthony's in the rear view.

Anthony knew Rick. He broke the stare.

They met Dr. Michaels at the hospital. Rick left Anthony with Chassity and he left Mo in the back on the floor. He drove, she blacked out.

DeBAITed Deaths Unknown Face

BRENDA

Three days had passed. Brenda had not seen anyone since Rick and Chassity had driven her as close to her home as possible without going out of their way. Chassity pushed a fifty dollar bill down Brenda's back pocket when she hugged her and told her to think about things. Rick had held the horn, causing a scene at the BP station where they left her standing next to the pay phone. He pulled off in the truck before Chassity closed the door. She was humiliated when she had to call a taxi to pick her up from Cleveland Avenue. Her cab fare was $49.43 by the time she reached the north side of Atlanta. Once she reached her door step, she was relieved, then deceived. When she flipped the switch to turn on the lights, they had been disconnected. Everything had remained in David's name. Everything in David's name disappeared. Her debit/credit cards, car, utilities, and her name. She spent the night in the dark, quiet, cool mini mansion. She curled up on the couch and slept in the clothes she had worn that day. The morning after, she answered the knock at the door.

"Mrs. Brenda Jones-Carter?" the young businessman asked.

"Yes, I am she," Brenda replied.

"You've been served," the businessman announced and then he turned and walked away.

She whispered as she read, "Divorce Papers. Oh God no! This isn't happening."

She sat on the kitchen counter. This was too much for her to bear. Three days alone in a cold, dark house, no money, no car, no friends, now this. The house had begun to settle, it smelled stale. She wore an oversized Ohio State sweatshirt, red sweat pants, and a pair of white sneakers. Her hair was matted down by hair gel. She looked a mess.

DeBAITed Deaths Unknown Face

The entire day and the next day she drank heavily, mumbled prayers, and drank again. On the counter next to her drink were two empty Patron bottles, a half-eaten sandwich and a prescription of Effexor. She rambled through the drawers and her cabinets. She began to feel like everybody was plotting against her; she felt as if she had failed a big test. She began to lose her mind. She grabbed the broom and began to scream, "STOP!!!" at the top of her lungs. She knocked down all four smoke detectors as she ran through the hallways, bedrooms, and the basement. She let herself go, she didn't care anymore. Now she sat in the kitchen floor with an empty bottle of Simply Sleep, an opened bottle of Effexor and two empty bottles of travel size Mr. Boston's vodka. She smiled. She cried. She dozed. She had given up. She wanted it to be over. She could no longer wait for her prayers to be answered. She did what she thought was best. She readily gave up.

*   *   *   *   *   *   *   *

"CLEAR!" the medical tech yelled. "CLEAR!" He yelled again.

She had a faint pulse. "Live Brenda! Damn!" "She has a pulse!" the female tech announced.

Brenda's body was safe. They next five days she remained in a semi-coma. Life continued for everyone else, she barely held on to hers. Her spirit spoke to her, sounding like a human voice. "It's okay." She opened her eyes and squinted from the lights. No one was there.

The nurse hurried into her room. "Mrs. Carter," she called. Brenda slowly blinked.

"Mrs. Carter!" the nurse called as she filled her pupils with light.

She coughed. Her body accepted her lungs. She opened her eyes.

DeBAITed Deaths Unknown Face

"The angels were with you Mrs. Carter. You gave us quite a scare," the nurse informed.

She understood that she was in the hospital. "What happened? How did I get here?" she asked.

"I'll go call your husband," the nurse announced.

"David?" she whispered.

"Yes, he found you just in time." The nurse left.

Brenda clutched the bed sheet. She moaned the words before she could speak them. "Jesus, thank you Lord."

She didn't cry. She wasn't afraid anymore. Being alone no longer scared her, being broke no longer bothered her. Starting over no longer haunted her. She had been set free. She smiled because she felt joy, she felt peace. The next couple of days passed and she had a series of medical tests. Doctors and counselors frequented her room. No calls, no visitors. She knew no one to call, she was content. The nurse called the number that David had left but no one ever answered. Still, the nurse or staff member always left a message. She had received the great news that she would be able to go home the next day. She didn't allow herself to think of 'her home.' That home was no longer her home. She found out that the social worker would help her seek contacts for a place to live. She called the shelter where she had worked for over seventeen years. They let her go over the phone, just as she had expected. David funded most of their programs although she had shares in the property.

All of her affairs were attached to this name. The battle was no longer worth losing the war. She decided that she would start all over. She wondered if anyone was looking for her. She wondered if she had been missed at all. She drifted off to sleep, her final night in the hospital. The next morning arrived; she showered and put back on the clothes that she wore the day she was admitted into the hospital. Her cab would be taking her to a shelter on the south side of

DeBAITed Deaths Unknown Face

Atlanta. She was determined to stick it out. She sat in the wheel chair and bid her farewells to a staff that had been very supportive. The elevator opened. She couldn't believe her eyes. There stood Chassity.

"How are you feeling?"

"So much better," Brenda replied.

"I got the messages. I'll take her," Chassity announced.

"Mrs. Carter do you know this person?" the medical tech asked.

"Yes, I will be fine. Thanks for everything Eddie. Take care."

"It's been a pleasure Mrs. Carter. You do the same."

He began to leave but he yielded at Chassity's voice.

"Do you mind wheeling her out to the car?" she asked, as she rubbed her arm that was still in a sling.

"My apologies. Sure no problem."

Brenda was thrilled to see Chassity; she would have been thrilled to see anyone that she knew, including David.

"Are you alone?" asked Brenda.

"Yes," Chassity replied.

"Let's go talk."

"The plans have already been made," replied Chassity as the tech wheeled Brenda into the elevator.

The elevator traveled 3 floors down within seconds. They detoured into the parking garage. Chassity escorted the tech to her rental car where he helped place Brenda in the front seat.

"So long and thanks again," Brenda said as she smiled and waved good bye. She felt like a new person. Her perspectives of people and things were clear to her. She accepted her faults and she finally appreciated the fact that living was enough. She finally understood that she still had lives to impact and a purpose to fulfill. She was satisfied being Brenda, even if it meant she had to be content with being Brenda Jones.

DeBAITed Deaths Unknown Face

"You mentioned that everything was already planned. How so? And what happened to your arm Chassity?" Brenda asked all at once.

"Let's just get you situated. I'll explain everything later," Chassity answered.

After they were settled in the car and on the road, Chassity pulled into the first fast food drive-thru she saw. She giggled before she looked to see Brenda's expression, but when she did, she was kind of surprised that Brenda's face wasn't twisted. The snob was gone. Brenda just sat still looking out of the window.

"Have you ever eaten Arby's before?" Chassity asked.

Brenda realized what Chassity had insinuated. She giggled too. "I don't think so, but I will try whatever you are having."

Chassity ordered them both the Roast Beef sandwich combos; they had it with curly fries and Jamocha Shakes. She pulled to the next window to pay for the food and received the order. Brenda took the bag and placed the drinks in the cup holder.

"Where are we going now?" Brenda asked again.

"Chill okay. "D" is not going to see you. Besides he is at the transitional home. He decided to finish his condition there instead of being on house arrest," Chassity blurted out, assuming that was the reason Brenda seemed to be in a hurry.

"No one mentioned David but you. I didn't expect to see him. I was only wondering."

Chassity accessed interstate 75-South. She drove without speaking.

"Why are we headed to Morrow?" Brenda asked.

"Your apartment is there and this rental is paid till the end of next month. You will be okay for a little while. You might as well eat. We have a ways to ride before we get there," she advised.

DeBAITed Deaths Unknown Face

Brenda was hungry and she knew that the day would be long and full of surprises. That was her life now, it was their mentality. She chewed the roast beef sandwich as if her life depended on it. She hurled her fries down 3-4 at a time and Chassity thought she was going to take the top off her Jamocha shake.

"Slow down," Chassity giggled.

"This is so good! I can't believe you paid $6.00 for this. Mmmm, thank you," Brenda mumbled, as she devoured the meal and licked her fingers.

Chassity was tickled and amused. "Sure, anytime. You can have mines if you want," she offered.

"I might eat it later if you really don't want it," Brenda replied.

Brenda cleaned up the fast food wrappings and then brushed the crumbs away. She sat up and then pulled the passenger vanity mirror down to see herself.

"Whoa! Why didn't you tell me I looked like this?" she screeched.

"I thought you knew."

"No, I didn't. Chassity, what am I going to do? I don't have anything. Don't get me wrong, I am willing to start over. I am ready to pick up the pieces. I just don't know how. I'm almost fifty years old. I don't know how to start over at my age."

Chassity sighed. "I know it will take some time, but "D" will give you what is rightfully yours. He is a lot of things, but he is not a thief."

Brenda nodded in agreement. "What about now though?"

Chassity looked at her stepmother. "You remember when I first came to live with y'all?"

Brenda nodded.

"Mama had just kicked me out and "D" told me that if I went to school, graduated, and made it to college, that he would take care of the rest."

DeBAITed Deaths Unknown Face

Brenda nodded again. "I remember."

"He didn't try to control me and anything I wanted to explore he let me. I just had to do my part. Just do your part for you," Chassity explained.

DeBAITed Deaths Unknown Face

MONIQUE

She had shot Chassity almost two weeks prior. Now she felt relieved after speaking to her mother briefly about her children. She dangled from the side of the bed still holding the phone. Ashton and Alex were doing well. They were under the impression that their mommy was out of town on business. Their lives were back to normal. School, video games, and baseball, most of the things they expected. However, she had been beaten badly, she was near death. Her eyes were blackened, her ribs were bruised, she had a cracked jaw, and a broken finger. Days had passed before she felt the missing patch of hair in her head. Her hair had been scalped from the root in the crown of her head and she wanted to die but couldn't. She dropped the phone on the side of the bed.

Afterwards, she still heard her mothers' voice. "I don't know what it is you're going through, but get passed it baby. These boys need their mother to raise them. Get past it Monique. I love you."

Rick sat in a chair next to a window that he had cracked for a smoke. They were alone in a cabin far back from the road, minutes from all the interstates, secluded from the rest of the world. Her face was swollen, she was unrecognizable. Her eyes moved over to Rick. He smoked as he stared at her. His face was warm, his eyes were pained. He loved her deeply but he had allowed these things to happen to her. He knew she wanted to know why. He knew that he had to tell her why. Not for her sake, but for the sake of his son, her boys. He knew she needed peace, he knew she had learned a valuable, priceless lesson. He finished his cigarette, blew the last exhale out of the window, and threw out the butt before he sealed the window. He took his chair, slid it across the room close to the bed where she rested.

DeBAITed Deaths Unknown Face

Mo remembered the fight. She remembered the shooting but she didn't remember the beating. The night they returned from the hospital, the nanny Liz, Naja's former girlfriend, had already packed the bags for the boys. She waited in the van before she followed Rick and Monique into the house. That night Rick shared an intense glare with Liz. No words were exchanged. Liz had her orders. Monique was beaten as she slumped over the bathtub nearly dead. Rick concealed his anger. He spoke clear, strong words in his mind, but a raspy whisper is what she heard.

"I didn't do this to you," he said.

Monique was silent, she heard his words and she already knew in her heart that he didn't do it. She nodded and asked, "Why?"

She wanted to know why she had to endure so much? Why were so many people involved?

Rick sighed and took her hand. "It's business," he replied.

Tears flowed down Monique's face.

"Naja?" she asked.

He knew what she meant and what she wanted to know.

"How?" she asked.

Rick knew that he could trust her. He knew that she would listen. He felt that she would understand. Or maybe he allowed himself to feel that way. He chose his words carefully.

"I slept with her. She used you Mo."

Mo was oblivious to his words. She began to shake her head in disbelief. She did not want to believe what he was saying to her.

"No," she mumbled. "No, Naja wouldn't do that to me," she cried. "Oh Rick, you wouldn't do that to me. How could you? WHO ARE YOU?"

"Listen, listen Mo, calm down. If "D" had found out that

DeBAITed Deaths Unknown Face

y'all were plotting to take all of his money, ruin his marriage, and control his life, he would have killed the boys, your folks, us, Monte and Naja."

He fell silent. He let his words settle in her mind then he spoke. "Do you understand?"

She nodded. "What about Chassity?"

Rick put his hand inside of Mo's.

"Naja never told you everything Mo. Chassity is David's daughter."

Mo gasped. She was shocked, her mouth sprung wide open and her eyes were open wide too. She looked like a raccoon. "WHAT?" Mo was in disbelief. "WHAT?" she yelled again.

"DING" Rick sang. She already had you pegged. That's why I blew her brains out. Naja had too much control and I was tired of her controlling you. You belong to me!" Rick yelled from brewing anger.

Mo became hysterical. "Oh My God! You what? Did you say that *you* killed Naja? No please *don't* say that!

He tried to make her understand. He had to make her listen. He didn't want her to hate him, he loved her. He panicked.

"Tell me what you said Rick. What happened? Please tell me," Mo cried.

Rick grabbed Mo's throat and stood over her. "It was either her or you," he whispered. I couldn't kill you Mo, so it had to be her." He held Monique's throat to keep control.

At first he held her neck without pressure and gazed into her eyes. He saw their bond disconnect through her eyes. She hated him and he knew it. He couldn't fathom the thought. At that moment he realized they would never be the family that he had hoped for. Monique panicked and Rick added pressure to her throat. She fought, his tears fell. She tried to speak as he gripped harder. She prayed to herself, *"Jesus is Lord over my salvation. Save me Jesus. Amen."*

DeBAITed Deaths Unknown Face

He kept pressing. Monique let go. He cried as she died underneath him. She was no longer moving. She died by his hands. *Damn!* Rick regained his focus as he realized what he had done. Instantly he wanted her back.

*   *   *   *   *   *   *   *

Sirens filled the air and helicopters swirled over the cabin. Rick didn't move. He couldn't move. Monte kicked in the door and ran down the hall into the bedroom where he saw his sister's body and his best friend on the floor.

"You killed her!" Monte screamed. "YOU KILLED HER MAN!" He became upset. Other officials ran into the room pushing Detective Monte Shaffer aside. They had to restrain him from harming Rick.

Rick didn't speak. He was set up, betrayed. It all came back around to him. The coroners came in to remove Monique's body.

Monte screamed out for his sister, "MO!!" He was too late. Their plan wasn't for her to die. He was devastated.

Rick was also devastated. He was immediately arrested for the murder of his ex-wife, the mother of his son, the woman he loved. The room had been wired. Orlando now had the evidence he needed. This matter was a deal in his favor. He set Rick up in exchange for immunity on pending charges.

Monte's colleagues comforted him as they urged him to leave the scene. He was offered the opportunity of notifying their family before the local news aired the story.

Monte accepted the offer and opted to drive to their parent's home alone. On his way there, he made a phone call to Chassity.

"Wassup?" she answered.

"Rick just killed Mo. He choked her to death."

"OH MY GOD!" Chassity screamed. Her emotions were cut short by his next statement.

DeBAITed Deaths Unknown Face

"You are going down in this too! I have the wire from Naja's car and I have the tap from her phone. You thought you and Rick were going to frame my sister but listen BITCH, you are going down too!"

Chassity began screaming hysterically and gave Brenda the phone.

"Hello? Who is this?" Brenda screamed.

Monte recognized her voice. Your stepdaughter is going down for MURDER!" Monte demanded. He snapped his phone shut.

Monte was hurt, he felt guilty. He and Mo were very close and now he was torn to pieces on the inside. Monte couldn't think of his nephews or Pops. He couldn't think of how her mother would feel. His heart ached; he began to blame himself as he wondered at what point he should have stopped things from spiraling out of control. He had been another truth in Monique's life. The hour long drive seemed to have been only ten minutes. He was pulling into his parent's driveway before he knew it. The boys were in the huge front yard playing soccer. They ignored his arrival due to the excitement of their game. Mama Lily sat in her rocking chair and rock as she crocheted, enjoying the view of the boys from the beautiful wide wrap-around porch on their split level home. Freddie stepped onto the porch as Monte eased up the steps, avoiding immediate eye contact.

"Monte?" Freddie called. "C'mon in boy. What brings you by in the middle of this Saturday morning?"

Monte stopped and kissed Mo's mother on her cheek.

"Can we talk inside?" he kindly asked, as he gestured to help her with her items.

"Is it about Monique?" her mother asked?

"Yes ma'am," Monte immediately answered.

DeBAITed Deaths Unknown Face

He knew from growing up in the house that he did not want her mother to get too worked up. They all sat in the den away from the front door in case the boys ran inside. There was a loveseat, two end tables, and a recliner chair in the room. The plasma television that hung over the fireplace was turned off. Freddie and his wife sat together on the love seat and Monte sat on the edge of the recliner chair. His demeanor changed from brother to business. He knew that his strength would be what they needed. He spoke with caution and compassion.

"Mo won't be coming back home." He paused to study her parent's faces. Freddie looked gloom. He knew. Her mother seemed uncertain and hopeful.

He continued. "Rick killed her." He stopped, no one spoke.

Freddie held his composure. In his mind he already knew, in his heart he already knew. Her mother began to cry, a daze crossed over her face as she nodded.

"Rick and another accomplice are also responsible for the death of Naja."

Freddie raised his eyebrows as he interrupted Monte.

"I don't believe this. You mean to tell me that boy killed both of my girls! What the hell is going on Monte? Boy, you'd better tell me something RIGHT NOW!" Freddie yelled and demanded.

"It's under investigation Pops. I don't have all the answers. He had Mo secluded. I wired the house for her safety. He confided in Mo about Naja but when Mo lost it, he went into a rage and choked her. I'm not sure if he realized what he'd done until it was too late."

Freddie sat in disbelief. He rested his arms on his knees and then he stood and left the room.

DeBAITed Deaths Unknown Face

Her mother continued to cry. "Go find out what happened Monte. I'm fine. I will find a way to tell the boys. Go on now, let us be," she whispered, as tears flowed down her face. Monte hugged her, she accepted it.

DeBAITed Deaths Unknown Face

DAVID

It was almost 11:30 am and David was a free man...well, sort of. He'd just signed himself out of the detention center. Once he walked from the parameters of the building, he powered on his cell phone. It immediately began buzzing. The voicemail was full. David had 32 unread text messages. He knew something was wrong. His heart throbbed. His mind told him to call Chassity, but he thought against it and called Anthony.

"What in the hell is going on?" he asked as soon as he heard Anthony answer.

"D, damn it man! This ain't good at all"

"Well, what is it? Spit it out!"

Anthony couldn't say it.

"What the hell is it?" David asked as he stood frozen in the middle of the road watching his bus pull off without him.

Anthony broke the news. "Rick killed Monique. It's all over the news and now they have a manhunt out for Chassity for Naja's murder," Anthony rambled.

"WHAT!" David replied. He felt like he was floating in outer space. There was a ringing sensation in his ears and a queasy feeling came over him. He fell to his knees. Bang! His phone dropped to the ground, he collapsed. A crack head across the street yelled out at him,

"AYE MAN, IS YOU OKAY?"

David didn't move. He was against the warm concrete heaving in disbelief. A counselor from the detention center was leaving for lunch when she saw his body in the middle of the road. She stopped the car, put it in park, and jumped out to help him. Anthony knew that David wouldn't be able to handle any of the news, that's why he held the phone line. "Hello? Hello? Is anyone on the line?" the counselor asked.

"Yes, I'm his brother. Get him to a doctor."

DeBAITed Deaths Unknown Face

"Okay, call me on my phone. I'll need your information," she insisted.

"What's the number?" Anthony asked as he paced back and forth in his townhouse.

"404-777-9311." She repeated it twice.

"I fucking heard you! Dial 911!" Anthony demanded.

David had only been released one week and one day. He chose to lay low right after his release. He had to be a good boy by completing his orientation at the half way house for ex-cons. The paramedics revived him on the scene; he had suffered an anxiety attack.

Anthony called the counselor. She gave him the hospital name. In route to the hospital, Anthony called Chassity. Brenda answered the phone for her.

"Hello?"

"Where is she?" he asked.

"She's right here."

"Hello?" Chassity cried.

"Listen. Change of plans. You stay there. Nobody knows where you are except Brenda, me and D. Tell Brenda to call me from her phone." He disconnected the call.

Brenda didn't have a phone. She had to leave Chassity alone to run to the pay phone at the store on the corner. She hurried. Chassity sat and cried in the closet the whole time she was gone.

"It's me." Brenda called to the silence on line.

"Look, "D" collapsed, he's at South Fulton."

"South Fulton?"

"Listen B! Focus, keep Chassity with you. Keep her safe until I get there. Don't watch the news. Get rid of her phone and tell her to clean herself up. Stay put!" He ended the call.

In the meantime, Jasmine continuously called Chassity's phone. Chassity ignored the call again. She began to scream out loud, "WHY IS THIS HAPPENING TO ME?"

DeBAITed Deaths Unknown Face

Jasmine called again. Chassity needed her. She needed anybody to save her. Finally she answered. Chassity sobbed, "Hello?"

Jasmine was sobbing too. "Is it true?"

They both knew it was true. They both knew that all of it was true. They cried together. "Jas, please, please, please, I need you. Oooh, I need you here with me. I'm so scared!" she cried.

"Why did he do that?" Jasmine cried. "Those poor boys. I'm with you Chassity. I'm with you, I'm with you, I'm with you," Jas whispered.

She cried for her friend. Brenda returned to the apartment.

"Hang up Chassity!" Brenda ordered.

"Brenda's here. I love you."

"I love you more," Jasmine replied.

Brenda snatched the phone and ended the call.

"We can't use your phone, they may be tracing your line. Anthony said for us to wait here. Go get that mess off your face, calm down and clean up baby."

Brenda was just as nervous and scared as Chassity. After all, she still hadn't faced David yet and she too was looking a mess.

"I have a bag of clothes in the trunk. There should be enough stuff for both us." Chassity continued to cry.

"Get in the shower. I'll go get whatever is in the trunk," Brenda called out as she headed out the door. She opened the trunk from the key chain. Her eyes bulged as she saw bags from Burlington's, Macy's, The Gap, and Dilliards. Then she connected the dots in her mind. She had zero dollars and Chassity seemed to be balling. That told her that she was 'on hold', with David and not disconnected. That was enough strength to make her smile. She gathered the bags and grabbed Chassity's back pack. She hurried back into the apartment and warmed up the meal they hadn't eaten from Arby's. When Chassity got out of the shower, she rushed

DeBAITed Deaths Unknown Face

into the shower to fix herself up.

"Chassity?" Brenda yelled out.

It startled her. "Yea," Chassity replied.

"It's not too late to pray. I've been doing it a lot lately and it is working in my favor."

Chassity didn't respond. She continued to get dressed. Brenda was out of the shower twenty minutes later. She took her time sorting the clothes. She matched an outfit that she felt was suitable to her taste, then she went through the back pack for beauty supplies. Once she finished her makeup she smiled and said, "Humble me, Lord," before turning the light off in the bathroom.

Chassity wore a white Apple Bottom t-shirt, fitted Apple Bottom jeans, with denim and white heels. Her face was clean, no piercings or weave covering her natural beauty. She had washed her hair, it was shoulder length and naturally curly. Chassity stood to be 5'3 with a petite frame. Her very fare complexion was from her African-American mother and David's Italian heritage.

"Smile?" Brenda asked.

Chassity took a deep breath and forced a smile.

Brenda walked over to her; she looked into her natural light brown-grayish eyes as she cupped Chassity's face into her hands.

"Look, we have been 'friends' long enough. You are in trouble and it's not too late for me to be a role model, to be a mother. I'm taking this chance Chassity because I love you. I love your father and this is our family. I need you to be strong because I haven't done this before, but I am here now and I promise to see you through this."

Chassity began to cry as she accepted Brenda's heartfelt plea. She felt vulnerable, she felt like a child.

"Thank you," Chassity said through her tears. She hugged Brenda and held her tight. "Please be my mommy, don't let anything happen to me," she begged.

DeBAITed Deaths Unknown Face

Brenda felt like crying too but she held her tears for Chassity. "Everything will be okay," she promised.

"Sit down and eat," Brenda said as she walked into the living room to peep out of the blinds.

She wore dark fitted Levi boot cut jeans, a solid black belt, a plain black fitted long sleeve shirt, with a pair of Chassity's black ankle high pointed toe boots. She too was more attractive dressed plain. Her skin, a shade lighter than Chassity's, complimented the blond streaks in her very short hair. She designed it into large curls all over her head; they looked wet but held their places. She kept watch out of the window while Chassity ate and engaged in conversation. Brenda began to take in the apartment, noticing they were on the 3rd floor. The apartment was small, but cozy and quiet. She noticed that it had already been furnished with a couch, love seat, matching end tables and oriental area rug. The kitchen was furnished with a 4pc table set, microwave, stove, and refrigerator.

She opened the refrigerator; it was already stocked with food just as the cabinets and pantry. She hurried back into the bedroom where she now observed the bed that she had ignored before, in addition to the 5pc dresser set and the plasma television that was mounted on the wall.

"Chassity, where are we?" she asked, as she walked back into the kitchen.

Chassity continued to eat as she looked up at Brenda. She chewed slower and then dropped her head.

"Chassity?" Brenda demanded.

"D" was going to stay here before…"

"Before what Chassity?" Brenda snapped.

"He was going leave you for Monique. He wanted to live here for a while," she mumbled.

DeBAITed Deaths Unknown Face

Brenda sat down at the kitchen table. She didn't speak. She leaned her face against her hands as she propped her arm on the table and took a deep breath. She thought to herself, '*He was actually going do it. After all those women and all these years, he finally had one that he was going to leave me and everything we shared together.*' She was in her own world contemplating the ways she imagined David telling her that he was leaving her for another woman.

Get it!" Chassity yelled. She had been talking to Brenda the last few seconds but Brenda hadn't heard her.

"Get what?" Brenda snapped back.

"The door," Chassity whispered as she ran back to the closet.

Brenda tipped toed over to the door and peeped out the hole. It was Anthony.

"Who is it?" she asked. She didn't want him to think she was being careless.

"Open the door 'B', he replied.

She did; he walked in and began talking immediately and fast. "D is coming here soon."

He didn't mention David's episode. Enough was already going on and he had to focus on the issues at hand now that he knew David was okay.

"He has to talk to you and Chassity. "CHASSITY?" he called.

Chassity came from the closet and gave Anthony a hug. He focused his conversation to her.

"Look, "D" will be here soon. You are going to have to tell him everything about all of this shit. That is the only way he is going to be able to help you. Nobody's gonna hurt you, nobody is going to take you away. Talk to "D" then call me. I'm going to meet with the lawyer now."

Okay," Chassity replied. He kissed her forehead and walked out of the door. He walked right back in before Brenda could lock the door.

DeBAITed Deaths Unknown Face

"Here," he said. He handed Brenda a box with a prepaid cell phone in it. "Use this, it's a minute phone so use it wisely and lock this door B."

Anthony left to go meet with the lawyer.

Brenda locked the door. She and Chassity sat on the couch each lost in their own thoughts. She couldn't believe she was about to see David for the first time in five years.

Chassity couldn't believe she was about to tell the truth about the entire mess she was in the middle of. She knew she had to, she couldn't lie to her father, she wouldn't. She was actually finally relieved. "Wow, wow, wow", she said repeatedly.

Brenda sighed. She was both nervous and excited at the same time. She too wanted to hear the truth. She prayed that she could handle the truth.

Chassity smiled, she felt reassured. "Well, get ready, get ready, get ready," she announced.

DeBAITed Deaths Unknown Face

JASMINE

Jasmine was very worried about Chassity. She couldn't believe the way things were unfolding. She was grateful that she made the decision to trust God and fell back when she did. She was in route to pick Shelton up from school, completely lost in her thoughts about Alex and Ashton. She also wondered if Rick would have killed her if she hadn't left when she did. She felt fortunate; she thought of her sister and realized that everything does happen for a reason.

"It could have been me," she said to herself. While she was sitting in line at Shelton's elementary school waiting for dismissal, David called her. She saw the area code and knew it was from Atlanta but she thought it was Chassity.

"Hey," she answered.

"Hey Jasmine, its David."

She was shocked. She didn't know that he was home or exactly the reason for his call.

"How are you?" she asked.

"I'm fine. It's been a long time hasn't it?"

"Yes sir, it has." She didn't know why she said 'sir' she just did. "D" had always intimidated her. She respected him.

"How is Shelton? Does he understand what has happened?" he asked.

"He has his good days. Other days he doesn't cry, he just drifts off into his own world. Whenever I ask him how he's feeling, he says he's okay."

"Does he seem confused?"

"No, he's not. He seems to be doing really good. I think we worry more about him and the situation more so than he does," she confided as she started the engine preparing to drive through the line to pick up her nephew.

"I need to meet with you very soon to discuss things for Shelton. You understand that don't you Jas?"

"Yes, that's cool."

DeBAITed Deaths Unknown Face

She stopped the car as she silently waved at the principal since she was still on the phone.

"I am picking him up now. Would you like to speak with him?" she offered.

David was on the line but he was speechless.

"Hello?" she called.

For the first time in a long time, things in his heart and in his life were changing. His mind was clear. He was emotional because he had never spoken to his son. He hadn't seen his son in five years. He took a deep breath.

"Yes," he answered.

He heard Jasmine tell Shelton that she had a surprise for him. "Your father is home in Atlanta, the place I used to live. He called to talk to you."

He heard Shelton ask, "So he's not locked up anymore and he can see me now? He really called me?"

"Take the phone", Jasmine said.

"Hello?" Shelton called.

"Shelton? Hey big guy. I'm your father, David."

"I know who you are. Have you seen me before?"

"Yes, of course I have. You were a baby but guess what?"

Shelton's smiled beamed as if David was standing in front of him.

"What?" he answered.

"I am going to plan a big play date for you and me. I will call your auntie really soon so that we can meet. Would you like that?" David asked, as he wiped his tears from his eyes.

"Yes, daddy. My mommy is an angel. She told me that you loved me. Do you daddy?" David could barely speak; he couldn't hold his tears anymore.

"Yes," he gasped. "Yes, you're my son and I love you."

"I love you too daddy. Here's auntie."

The next voice "D" heard was Jasmine's. Her voice cracked; she fought back her own tears as she smiled for her nephew and his father.

DeBAITed Deaths Unknown Face

"That went well," she said.

"Thank you," David replied. "Before you go Jasmine, I need to talk to you about something else."

Jasmine had felt it brewing. She had only hoped to escape it. "Chassity?" she suggested.

At that point "D" realized that Jasmine was unaware of 'his' relationship with Monique. "No, I will take care of Chassity. I wanted to ask you about Rick."

"Rick?"

"It's only you and Chassity now. I have to know that she is being honest with me. Tell me what you know, start with Rick."

"D" can you hold on a sec? Let me drop Shelton off at my parents so that I can talk alone."

"Go ahead. I need to know this now though Jas."

He held the line as Jasmine and his son exchanged kisses. "I'll be back in a few minutes, go in the house," he heard Jasmine tell Shelton.

"I'm back," she told "D."

"I'm listening."

"Me and Rick was cool at first. Naja told me that Rick had a thing for me. I really don't be into white boys or anything but Rick had a certain swagger. I admit that I was kind of feeling him too so we started kicking it on the low."

"So Naja told you Rick was into you, not Chassity?"

"Right." Jasmine was fearful but she didn't know why.

"Did you ever meet Monique?" he asked as he held his breath.

"A few times after me and Rick got tight. We started hanging out with the kids and stuff. She was always cool though. I didn't even realize that her sister Naja was the same Naja I knew. She had told me her sister was killed but Mo black and Naja white so it threw me off when I found out they were raised together. I didn't know Naja was adopted".

"Who is Bradley?"

DeBAITed Deaths Unknown Face

"Bradley? I don't know any Bradley."

"Bradley was seeing Naja." He pressed, picking Jasmine for information.

"As far as I know Naja was with Liz."

"Who is that?"

"Her girlfriend. Naja was into women lately."

"I appreciate your time sweetie. I will call you soon. Don't worry about Chassity."

"Tell her that I send my love and to call me."

"Okay." D ended the call.

DeBAITed Deaths Unknown Face

BRENDA

It had been almost two hours since Anthony left the apartment. Chassity was curled into the fetal position on the couch. Brenda sat in the chair sipping from bottled water. During their wait, they talked about future plans. Brenda reassured Chassity that everything would work out according to God's will. The comment didn't sway Chassity's feelings in any particular direction. She wasn't comforted because she wasn't sure of what God's will was. She knew that she was responsible for certain things and she expected to be punished for those things. On the other hand, she looked forward to dodging another bullet. She had one more year at Spellman where she intended to earn her degree and move as far away as possible.

Knock, knock, knock. He was there. David knocked at the door. Brenda jumped to her feet; she brushed her clothes off and whispered to Chassity,

"How do I look?"

Chassity winked and told her, "You better open the door before he has to knock again."

"Coming," Brenda called. "Peace be still" she prayed.

Brenda opened the door and David stepped in without speaking. Brenda closed the door and locked it. David looked very calm; he was very handsome standing at 6'4, solid as a brick. His head was bald, his beard had turned grey. His light brown eyes softened as Chassity stood to greet him,

"Welcome home, I missed you," she said as she hugged and squeezed her father.

"I'm glad to be home baby girl, just in time to be here for you."

He spoke lightly as he lifted Chassity during their hug.

"You look good David. Welcome back," Brenda complimented.

"So do you Brenda. It's good to be back," he replied.

DeBAITed Deaths Unknown Face

Brenda stepped forward to hug her husband. He accepted her advance. David hugged her with one arm wrapped around her waist. It wasn't what Brenda had hoped for but at least he acknowledged her.

"Are you hungry? Do you need anything?" she asked, regretting that she didn't take the opportunity to prepare him a home cooked meal.

"Not today, we won't be here long."

Brenda took her seat back in the chair. David sat on the edge of the couch next to Chassity facing both ladies.

"Come into the kitchen with me, both of you," he said.

The ladies filed out of the room, Chassity behind and Brenda in front of David. They all took a seat. David sat in the middle, Brenda to his left, and Chassity to his right,

"Listen, everything is out of whack. You two have lost complete control of almost everything that I have. We will get to that but right now we have bigger issues to deal with."

David looked at Chasity in the way a father looks at a daughter when she is in serious trouble. Chassity sat up straight and looked her father in the eye.

"Now Chassity, explain to me everything you know about everybody involved, including Brenda's affair."

He glanced between the two ladies. Brenda looked away to avoid eye contact,

"It seems to me that this all was masterminded. Now I have to figure out how to keep you out of jail for murder," he nodded at Chassity.

"And you," now nodding at Brenda, "for conspiracy to commit murder," he stated.

David placed a tape recorder on the table. "I know that you didn't kill Naja just like I know Brenda wouldn't have wasted my money to have her killed either. This will help all of us in the end, just be honest."

DeBAITed Deaths Unknown Face

Chassity took a deep sigh, she was nervous. She knew that she knew too much.

"Look Chassity, I am still under prison watch. We have to meet the lawyer. So unless you are ready to go to jail, press play and START TALKING!" he roared.

Brenda cleared her throat and sipped her water. Chassity looked at Brenda, she nodded. She looked at David, he glared back. She picked up the tape recorder, cleared her throat, and began to talk.

"When Jasmine told me that Rick was trying to kick it with her, I disapproved because of Rick's temper. But then she told me that Naja hooked it up. At first I thought it was odd, but the longer the relationship, fling, or whatever they had was going on, the more I watched them. I didn't get suspicious about anything until we were at Jasmine's house the day she found out about Tawanna's death. To me it looked like Naja and "O" had some sort of silent communication going on, but I didn't say anything about it to anyone."

David held up his hand. "Hold on, no nicknames. Who is "O"?

"Orlando."

He made a mental note.

She looked at Brenda for a response.

"The day Tawanna was killed, didn't you see the way Naja was acting?"

"I remember," Brenda replied.

"Later that night, Rick called me and told me that Naja had asked him to ride with her to the state line on business. He said Naja told him that they needed to talk."

David interrupted. "State line?" Why did Rick call you to tell you anything? I know why but I still need you to say it for the tape."

DeBAITed Deaths Unknown Face

She sighed, "I am your daughter and my position was to keep tabs on Brenda, Monique, DJ, Shelton, and Rick. I was supposed to make sure all of your business flowed and keep everybody in line. He called me because you told us to always watch each other's back. You told me to trust Rick because you had other people watching him."

She shifted in her seat. David noticed.

"Well, he called me and told me that Naja wanted him to ride out with her. He said she needed a favor and the favor was to help setup Brenda."

Chassity paused. She saw Brenda's eyes squint with anger. She knew Brenda was getting upset.

"Go on," David urged. "How did they plan to get my money without my consent?" he asked.

"At the time Rick didn't have all the information. I told him to call Naja to tell her that he would go. Me and Rick had planned to get it on tape and then find out how you wanted to handle it. Anyway, he got Naja to rent the rental car. When she picked him up, he told her to stop at the Chevron off Old National. He sent her in the store to pay for gas and that's when he put the wire in the car. I was in the parking lot behind the store waiting on them to pull out. I flashed my lights so that he knew that I could hear the tap in the rental that I had. That's when I found out that Naja had already told Monique about Brenda. Monique and Naja set it up for Brenda to sleep with Monte; he seduced her, for his sisters, so they say. Naja was talking about how she had invested years into taking your money. She basically hated Brenda enough to bring her to her knees.

"What happened?" he asked Chassity.

DeBAITed Deaths Unknown Face

Chassity gave her version of the story. "I heard a loud noise through the wire. Rick had slapped Naja and the car swerved off the road. That's when I started flashing the lights signaling him to get out. He got out and I picked him up. He kept telling me that he was gonna have to kill her cause she talked too much and that she put his boys in jeopardy by crossing you. He and Naja were sleeping together behind Monique's back. Oh yea, and Freddie supposedly had Brenda thinking that he was gonna leave his wife so Rick was mad because he felt like the whole family was in on it, except Monte. It pissed me off because I felt like everybody was taking advantage of my family. Rick said he had to take her out before she got everybody killed. I told him that I didn't want to have any part of it, but she was still on the side of the road when we were about to pass by her. Rick told me to pull up behind her so that he could get his phone and the wire. I stopped but when I saw him point a gun at her I started to pull off. He jumped in the truck while I was pulling off."

"WHOA! Time out, time out here," David interrupted. "So you are telling me that Rick killed Naja?"

"Yes, he did. I saw him."

David looked at Brenda. Something wasn't making sense.

"I thought someone said that she was with a guy named Bradley?"

"I know about that too," Chassity stated. She began to explain. "When the local police and Monte, Monique's brother, talked to Monique about Naja's investigation, she told them that Naja was with Bradley, but Naja was really with Rick. Naja lied to Monique because she had been seeing Rick behind her back. She used her coworker 'Bradley's' name only to throw Mo off."

David was breathing heavy. "Damn it! I can't believe this. I just can't believe any of this!" he blurted.

"Well it is the truth," Chassity reassured.

Brenda looked over at David, her tone was persuading.

DeBAITed Deaths Unknown Face

She kept her voice calm, "I'm not proud of any of my mistakes, but I will admit to an affair with Freddie, and after a few drinks, I did also allow myself to fall astray with Monte. The things that Chassity knows did not come from me. She actually knows more about the situation than I do," Brenda confided.

David was relieved but he wasn't going to show either of them any sign of acceptance for all the hell they had allowed to break loose.

He dismissed Brenda's comments for the time being. He needed to know more.

"Fast forward to Monique's death. What happened there?" David grilled Chassity for more answers.

Chassity revealed more information. "After Rick shot Naja, I told him that I was going to visit you in prison to tell you what happened in person, but he told me if I did that he would kill me too."

David jumped to his feet. "WHAT THE HELL?" He shouted.

"David." Brenda spoke softly as she stood to massage his shoulders. "Calm down, she's here, let her finish."

David allowed Brenda to massage him. He took another deep breath then sat back down in his chair.

Chassity continued on. "He told me not to say anything, to let him figure out a way to handle Monique. He kept saying that he couldn't let anything happen to her boys, especially his son. He told me that Monique and Ashton were all he had and he couldn't let anything happen to his family. He didn't believe that Monique was guilty of anything; he knew that Naja had planned it all. He knew what people would believe. He seemed so worried about your reaction and his obligations to you. He kept telling me that I didn't understand his position in the matter. I didn't know what else to do. So I told Orlando the whole situation."

That hit a nerve.

DeBAITed Deaths Unknown Face

David didn't like that. "Why him?" he asked.

Chassity suddenly realized how careless she had been. She cleared her throat before she spoke,

"Because that's who I've been seeing. I thought that by Monte being his step brother that maybe he would tell him more about the situation."

Good answer. David believed it. "Did he?" asked David.

"No, Monte never confided in Orlando as far as I know or could tell, but Orlando got real mad. He said that he felt like Rick was in on it since he was sleeping with Naja. He said that Rick was the one deceiving everybody, not just Monique."

That even made David doubt Rick.

"Orlando asked me when Freddie came into the picture. I told him that I didn't know."

David shifted to look at Brenda.

Yep, her turn. "When did Freddie come into the picture?" David asked Brenda.

He pulled her arm from around his neck. His demeanor changed with Brenda but Chassity got sympathy because he saw her as his innocent, sweet daughter. Brenda caused him to hurt. As his wife, he expected more, but she cheated. She let him down. In spite of all that he had done against her, David trusted Brenda more than he loved her. He became serious.

"Sit back down. Now tell me, when did Freddie come into your life?" he demanded.

Brenda was no fool. She knew David would not wait half of a second before all hell broke loose. She spoke up quickly.

"Three years ago, but we weren't intimate until about a year ago," she answered.

DeBAITed Deaths Unknown Face

David looked at Brenda, he sucked his teeth. For a second, he contemplated slapping the snot out of her but he didn't. He turned his focus back to Chassity who was still trying to defend her boyfriend Orlando. She was a fool for Orlando's love. She loved him enough to stand up to her father. Chassity began with what she thought David would ask.

"Orlando's whole thing was that he knew Rick didn't like him. He knew that Rick considered him to be a snitch."

"He is," David confirmed. He chuckled to himself, another mental note.

Chassity ignored the accusation. She kept digging her own hole.

"Well, Orlando called Anthony and gave him the information about what was going on. They confronted Rick while I was in South Georgia with Jasmine for Tawanna's funeral. When I got back, Brenda had already been questioned. Every time anything took place, Rick or Orlando called me. Rick was getting his information from Monte and Orlando was too so I was getting the whole scoop while I was out of town. Anthony decided that the situation had gotten out of control."

David interrupted! "Finally! Somebody was thinking with a damn brain!"

Chassity sounded desperate. "He told Rick to get Monique out of the city, to make her leave. Find somewhere to go and start over but Monique didn't want to do that."

Chassity was crying. She continued to speak through her tears, passed her guilt.

Mo didn't want to change her life or move her children out of the blue, so Rick took her to that cabin to scare her into leaving town. Everything was cool; she even called Brenda to apologize about everything. Orlando and Rick recorded that conversation on tape too because Monique called from Monte's phone. Orlando told me that Monte also sent a copy of the conversation to Anthony's cell phone.

DeBAITed Deaths Unknown Face

All of this happened the day you had Brenda's car towed."

Surprise! "What?" David yelled. "I never had Brenda's car towed!"

Bing! Brenda was back. "What about my debit cards, credit cards, the lights, and the divorce papers?" she rambled off.

David was dumbfounded. "I didn't arrange for any of those things to happen. Let's get back to all these other things later. Chassity finish this up, we have to leave in a few minutes."

Chassity carried on. "Okay, anyway, Rick didn't drop me off at Orlando's after we left Brenda at the gas station."

David was thinking that he had heard it all. Now it sounded like she was going deeper. He was just shaking his head at all the foolishness that had taken place.

She continued with her antics. "Instead, he took me to the cabin and told me to scare Mo with my gun, convince her to leave and I did."

That part was a lie but it sounded good. She kept talking. "Mo agreed to leave but then she attacked me. That is why I had on that sling."

Chassity looked at Brenda, then to David. She knew she would have to reveal her part, in order for them to believe the rest.

"During my fight with Mo, the gun went off and I was shot in the shoulder. Another bullet grazed my ear."

David interrupted, "SHOT!" YOU WERE SHOT? Where the hell was Anthony? How in the hell did he let you get shot!"

David almost had a heart attack, he was very upset!
Brenda was frozen in her seat.

DeBAITed Deaths Unknown Face

Now Chassity couldn't believe that she was actually going to kill Monique. It all had seemed so worth it. She heard his question, but she was lost in her thoughts. *'I could have stopped Rick from killing Naja, and I probably could have saved Mo's life too. Oh, my God!'*

"Answer me. Where was Anthony?" David asked again, as he grew impatient.

"He was there. He and Rick took me to the hospital. He stayed with me the entire time. Rick took Monique back to the cabin. Orlando told me that Monte would make sure that he and Liz would see no jail time for their cooperation. Orlando called Rick to find out what happened to me. Rick explained how I was shot and Orlando told Rick that he better make sure Monique paid for what she did to me or else it would look like he really was in on their plot. Rick preferred that another woman handle it and since Liz was there playing nanny, he decided to let her be the bad guy. At least it would keep Monique alive. Rick didn't know the cabin had been wired by Anthony and Orlando to prove that he put me up to scaring Mo with a gun. They paid Liz to beat Monique. Afterwards, Rick went back to the cabin. He pretended like he was so upset about what happened. While he was out, Monte told Monique to get Rick to confess to killing Naja. Anthony threatened Monte to clear my name or else he was going over Monte's rank with all the evidence and a jury could decide. Monique got Rick to confess, but...."

Chassity became choked up. Hearing herself explain her version of the events made her see that none of it was worth it. Her words made her realize how selfish she had been. Her words changed her perspective about everyone, even Orlando. Still her heart was not ready to admit that.

DeBAITed Deaths Unknown Face

"Mo"…she started up again. Her heart was aching for Monique. "She… it was too much. Monique couldn't handle hearing the truth. I guess Rick couldn't handle it either, so he snapped and they got it all on tape."

David was standing on his feet pacing very slowly across the floor. He heard Chassity press stop, the tape recorder clicked. Chassity left the room. Brenda remained seated, tears ran down her face. David was at odds with himself. He couldn't believe that what he had and who he was had impacted so many lives. Brenda cried because she realized how hatred turned into greed, lust, envy, murder and revenge. She wondered how things would have turned out had they been handled differently years prior. David looked at Brenda for the first time with soft eyes, the way a husband looks at his wife. She shared his stare. She stood.

"It's okay," she whispered.

David stopped pacing. He stopped in front of Brenda. He looked at her and took in her beauty. He knew they were different somehow, someway. He hugged her, she felt his feelings. Her emotions cried for him.

"This is my fault," David admitted. He no longer held his tears.

DeBAITed Deaths Unknown Face

MONIQUE

Now her mother rubbed her temples. "O Lord, please help me to understand," she prayed. She spoke whispers into the empty kitchen. "Mo baby, I miss you already. Tell me what to do with the boys. Show me how to get through this." Her mother heaved. Her heart had been shattered into over a million pieces.

Monte pulled into the driveway to check on things. He wanted to see his nephews. He let himself in the house and saw his stepmother in her despair at the kitchen table. He didn't speak. He kneeled down on the floor beside her. He began to rub her back. His stepmother turned her head to face him. She saw in him the eyes of her daughter.

"Monte?" she humbly called. "Sit with me," she invited.

He stood to sit in the chair at the table beside her. His eyes were full of tears, rage poured through his veins. He missed his sister. He was enraged but his stepmother had a way with words.

She caught him by surprise when she asked, "How is Rick?" in her sweetest tone.

He couldn't answer. He could only cry. After a while he cleared his throat. He struggled to answer. "He is in custody but he isn't talking."

She nodded her head, she wasn't surprised.

"Mama Lily, I don't understand enough of this mess to explain to you yet. But I promise to raise my nephews. They can live with me if they need too." he offered.

"Shhh...not now. Let's not go down that road now. I'm not ready," she kindly replied.

His cell phone rang. He answered. "Hey Pops, I'm already here. No, everything is okay. She's fine; the phone is just off the hook. I'll be here a while."

DeBAITed Deaths Unknown Face

Monte concluded his conversation with Freddie. He spoke to his stepmother. "Are the boys here or with Pops?" he asked.

"He took them to my sister's house away from everything for a while. They don't know anything yet."

Monte sat quietly. He couldn't imagine how the boys were going to handle the news much less understand it. He was having an extremely hard time understanding exactly what happened himself.

"Do you need me to make calls or do anything?" Monte asked.

"Not today. Today, my baby left this cold, cold world. I just want to sit here and think about my baby today," she calmly replied.

Monte knew that there was peace over his stepmother. He was relieved as he studied her movements and listened to her words. He realized that she was conscious of what she was saying and doing. The way she sat so still, remained so calm, and spoke so softly revealed her peace. Back in his youth he had moved into their home his junior year of high school. When he first moved in, he was rebellious. His stepmother Lily was patient and firm. She kept him in line and guided him into the man he had become. He respected her deeply.

Interrupting his thoughts, she asked, "Are you still leading Naja's investigation?" She searched his eyes.

He knew he had to answer. "No ma'am. I am on administrative leave."

Her eyes saw everything that he wanted *his* eyes to hide.

DeBAITed Deaths Unknown Face

DAVID

"Let's go Chassity!" Anthony shouted.

They were running late for her appointment with the defense attorney. David decided to have Brenda drive for him. The stress of the situation, plus all the information had taken a toll on him. Anthony and Chassity followed in Anthony's car.

"What side of town are we headed to?" Brenda asked.

"Main Street, College Park," David replied.

Brenda seldom visited the South side of Atlanta. It just wasn't her cup of tea. However, today she was grateful for the forty-five minute drive. To her that meant she could be alone with her husband.

Chassity finally came out of the bathroom. She had been crying and had taken some time to pray. She had confessed that she had done a lot of wrong things and admitted that she didn't want to go to jail. She promised that if the Lord saw her through, that she would turn her life around. David locked up the apartment and they all hit the road.

As Brenda drove, he inhaled her natural fragrance. He appreciated the fact that she was still by his side, though he was still reluctant to feel for her. The current disaster still wasn't enough to make him look past her indiscretions.

"What happened out here Brenda?" David asked.

"What do you mean?" she replied as she focused on the road.

She drove. He watched her drive as he spoke.

"You, Chassity, the fellas. What the hell happened? The bottom fell out all of a sudden."

She didn't respond. He was quiet. David was in disbelief that every woman who had a key role in his life was either dead or potentially headed to jail. Brenda remained silent. She knew he was venting.

DeBAITed Deaths Unknown Face

He kept thinking about everything that had taken place. His mind was cluttered; his head was beginning to ache. Everything and everyone was worrying him.

"Damn!" he said to himself at the thought of losing her.

"Were you really trying to kill yourself or was that just another one of those attacks you have?" he asked Brenda.

At first she was silent, he had caught her off guard. She was glad he asked.

"I was afraid to live but I didn't want to die either," she answered.

She looked over at him. He squeezed his eyes tight and let the passenger window down. He took a long deep breath before he spoke.

"I'm too old for this. None of this was supposed to happen."

Brenda remained silent. She knew him better than he knew himself. His heart ached for Monique and Brenda knew it.

"I'm to blame for all of this. I should have just told the truth about everything from the beginning."

Monique had told him time and time again to tell the truth. She tested his trust, love, and will power. Even more dangerously, she tested his manhood. He now understood that Mo knew everything but he passed the opportunity to show her the respect and love she looked for from him. He had convinced himself that Monique would have changed things involving Naja and maybe she would have done things differently. Maybe Rick or Chassity or anyone else wouldn't have reacted in the ways that they did. Guilt was eating David alive.

Brenda spoke, "God is trying to tell you something David. Just be patient, he will reveal it to you. You're still standing for a reason."

DeBAITed Deaths Unknown Face

Brenda's words comforted David, although he still felt anger towards her. He wanted her, he loved her, he just couldn't get past the fact that she admitted to having an affair. He couldn't get past the point of wondering if she would have willingly made it known if it had not been for Monique. He thought of all his actions. His revelations overwhelmed him. The fact that Brenda was really clueless of Monique was now an obvious blessing. God saw fit for his wife to be left on this earth to comfort him. Yet, he still longed for his mistress. They were about ten minutes away from their destination. Brenda tapped the brakes. Something was wrong. Anthony was pulling his car over onto the median. She followed over into the median behind him. He jumped out of his car. Now he was running towards David and Brenda. He stopped on the passenger side to speak with David. Using their cells was too risky, they were probably tapped. This could not wait. He was all out of breath.

Anthony heaved as he rushed his words. "D, they want Chassity to come to Pryor Street. Frells is already down there waiting on her. He's Chassity's lawyer. He says he will take the tape when we get there. We have thirty minutes before the Marshalls takeover."

"THE MARSHALLS!" David yelled.

Anthony was angry. "Yea, Monique and Naja are relatives of a lead detective. Monte has been put on administrative leave. It's no surprise that Rick isn't talking. If Chassity isn't being straight up, she could go down with Rick in this!"

David nodded. He couldn't speak. He rolled up his window.

Brenda continued to follow Anthony. She prayed silently to herself. *'Lord, have mercy. I am trusting in you to see our family through. If you must use us to get the glory, then have your way. Amen.'*

DeBAITed Deaths Unknown Face

She reached over the arm rest and took her husband's hand. He squeezed it and didn't let go. He held on tightly as she drove. Minutes later, they were parked in the parking lot and getting out of their cars.

"Let's pray before we go in there," she suggested.

Anthony looked at Brenda as if she was crazy.

"D" nodded. He eased over to hold Brenda's hand. Chassity grabbed her father's hand. She rested her head on his chest. They looked over at Anthony, waiting for him to join. Anthony leaned against the car.

"Go ahead, Jesus is everywhere," he said.

David chuckled at Anthony's sarcasm.

Brenda ignored Anthony and began to pray. *"Lord, we are standing in the need of your mercy and your grace. Forgive each of us for our sins. Have your way Lord. Let no weapons formed against us be able to prosper. In the name of Jesus, Amen."*

"Amen," said Chassity and David.

"Amen sister," Anthony teased.

Anthony spotted the defense attorney immediately. He introduced everyone.

"David, this is an old friend of mine, Maynard Frells. He has agreed to represent Chassity."

He pointed to each of the ladies. "This is her stepmother Brenda and of course this is Chassity."

The family all took turns shaking hands with Mr. Frells. His deep, sophisticated voice greeted them. "I intend to do the best I can. Let's get started please. Follow me to the conference room."

Once inside and seated around the round table, he advised they had no time to waste. He insisted on hearing the tape immediately. Anthony pressed play, Mr. Frells listened carefully.

DeBAITed Deaths Unknown Face

The details of Chassity's statements were critical to his defense. He too was amazed by the deceit in the evidence. Chassity stuck to the facts surrounding each death that she knew about. If she had mentioned the entire connection of everybody, including her parents, a different story may have been painted. Of course she knew that. She told only what she wanted to tell. Those details would never be heard in open court. The tape played for about forty five minutes. The authorities waited, aware that Chassity was in the building meeting with her lawyer. That held them off. It would also provide her an opportunity to turn herself in.

Mr. Frells clicked off the tape. His voice was strong. "Well, what we have here is strong evidence in your favor. You've explained how and why Rick Shaw murdered the victims. We will keep this to ourselves for now. Do you have the recordings from the wiretap from Ms. James' vehicle?"

"Yes, this is it. Here," Anthony answered handing the small tape to the attorney.

Mr. Frells put the small tape into a plastic bag and then inserted it into the pocket of his briefcase. He turned to Chassity. "I will be with you during the entire interrogation process. Do not go into details about anything unless I advise you to. Stick to the facts, if you are uncomfortable about answering any question, do not answer. Rick Shaw has not given any statement to the authorities. You have to be very careful how you handle yourself. Are you ready?" Mr. Frells instructed.

"Yes," Chassity replied. She hugged her family before leaving the room.

The counselor who found David collapsed in the middle of the road that morning had called his parole officer. Anthony had her meet him at the hospital. Once there, David explained the circumstances regarding his children, Shelton and Chassity. His parole office approved conditional parole for David. He had not told anyone of his changes due to the

DeBAITed Deaths Unknown Face

way the day transpired.

"I have to be home by 11 pm. The apartment is my approved address and Brenda has to accompany me at the apartment since it was put in her name."

Brenda spoke up, "You mean to tell me that you put the apartment in my name?" she asked with an accusing tone.

She was offended because she knew that David planned to leave her for Monique and live there in the meantime.

"I had to. It was easier at the time, besides you had the house occupied. Now say something else," David stated.

His arrogance put her back in her place. Brenda stood and walked to view the city from the window; removing herself from David's presence for a while. Anthony took advantage of their freedom. He got straight to business with David. He kept his tone low.

"How do you want to handle Rick?"

"I'm not worried about Rick," David said.

Anthony had more news to reveal, a few pieces that Chassity left off of the tape. He continued. "D, Chassity called Monique the night Naja was murdered. She was on the scene with Monique right after she got the news about Naja. She didn't mention any of that in the tape."

"How do you know?" David asked.

"O", Anthony replied.

David remained silent. He had put his daughter in harm's way unintentionally. He realized that he made her a target for corruption.

"Damn!" he whispered.

David had escaped many scenarios in the past. He had jumped through countless hoops of flames but he couldn't see past the depths of this ordeal. Brenda overheard them. She looked over her shoulder, glanced at both of them, then continued to look out of the window at nothing in particular.

"Did you cut her off?" David asked Anthony.

DeBAITed Deaths Unknown Face

"Yea, you told me to do what I had to do. At the time I didn't feel like she would pull through, so I cut her off."

"You almost killed her too."

He realized that he was just as much to blame for her nervous breakdown.

"I'll take care of it," Anthony replied.

"What about the divorce papers? How did you have those served?" David questioned.

"That was Naja. They almost thought of everything."

"Except dying," David replied. "I need you to have Shelton and Jasmine brought into town for a visit."

"Okay."

David was growing impatient. He stood and stretched.

"She's been back there too long."

"Give it a few more minutes. The press is all over this," Anthony advised.

Brenda returned to her seat, the guys stopped talking. David sat back in his seat. Mr. Frells returned... alone.

"WHERE IS SHE?" David yelled.

Mr. Frells held his hand up. "Calm down Mr. Carter, let me explain. They have a witness who has given a statement against Chassity. His name is Orlando Baitess. He snitched. Her boyfriend ratted on her."

David looked at Anthony. They transpired thoughts through each other. Brenda looked away. She couldn't take it.

Frells continued, "Mr. Baitess is claiming that Chassity helped mastermind the plot against Ms. James and her sister Ms. Blake, Monique's maiden name. He claims that Chassity found out about the plot through Rick Shaw. Says she became obsessed with seeking revenge against the deceased. He also claims that your daughter confided in him about the plot; however, Orlando Baitess is the star witness for the D.A. His loyalty is with his step brother, Detective Montavious Shafer."

DeBAITed Deaths Unknown Face

"UNBELIEVABLE!" David yelled.

"This is not happening," Brenda uttered.

Anthony couldn't move. He never saw this turn of events coming.

David dropped his head. He couldn't look at any of them. What are her charges?"

Mr. Frells answered. "Well, as of now she is facing two counts of first degree murder, two counts of conspiracy to commit murder, two counts of aggravated assault, and one count of simple battery.

DeBAITed Deaths Unknown Face

BRENDA

Brenda looked over at her worried husband, she rubbed his back. Their connections made arrangements for a weekend pass for David to be with his family during their crisis.

David avoided eye contact at first. He still felt some resentment and guilt about the entire ordeal. She slid deeper into the sheets to hold him.

After hours of contemplating her words she finally spoke. "Honey, I need you to forgive me."

He didn't respond, so she kissed his lips softly. He kissed her back.

"I love you," she whispered.

"Yea, well show me," he replied.

She gazed into his eyes, he winked. He pulled her closer as he held her under his arm.

"I want to change," David confided.

She tried to move, but his weight rested upon her.

"Listen to me," he continued. "When I was in prison, I met a man who lost his entire family during a home invasion. His wife and two daughters were murdered. Now he is doing life for retaliating. I want to let this go "B". No more... I can't."

His words trailed off as he cried, resting his face in her neck.

As her tears trickled down her face, she whispered, "Thank you Lord," as she held her husband.

He began to kiss her neck, then her nipples. She guided him with her fingers as she caressed his back. David rose up from kissing her belly. He looked Brenda in her eyes. "I am in love with you and for the first time in my life, this is real to me. I feel like God is trying to tell me something and I want to listen to him. I know you are my wife for a reason. I see that now. I love you Brenda."

DeBAITed Deaths Unknown Face

She remained silent, appreciating his words. Her husband removed her panties and kissed her thighs. Revisiting her softness, he buried his face in the center of her body as he licked her buried treasures. She anticipated him as she moaned from his pleasure. He rolled her over and parted her legs and guided her bottom to his chest. As he lowered her to his lips, the sensational insertion made her pant. David took it slow as he indulged himself. Hours passed as their spirits reconnected. She sat on his thick anatomy as she climaxed while grinding on top of her husband. He sucked her nipples while holding her ass. She rode him slowly as she turned to a backwards position, leaning back into his chest while his fingers explored with her pink girl. She gasped as she leaned forward and gently increased her speed. As he squeezed her thighs, he slapped her ass. When his body jerked from the reach of his peak, she screamed. He held her in place, as they climaxed in unity.

That night they vowed never to be apart again. David finally decided to leave the game. The night was cool and the coziness of the apartment snuggled their warm bodies deeper into the black satin sheets that were fitted against the soft, large king sized mattress. He wrapped his arms around her waist as he held her close. Brenda knew that his tears were for all of them. She knew that he needed to be loved through his turmoil. She had forgiven him and he had forgiven her. They vowed to stand together.

She kissed him. "It will be alright in the morning," she whispered.

Brenda got out of bed around 6:30 am the next morning. She prepared pancakes, bacon, eggs and grits for David. The coffee was freshly brewed; she poured fresh juice and carried the arrangement into the bedroom. She was his superwoman! She had her swagger and her man back!

DeBAITed Deaths Unknown Face

He turned on the television as the news station announced, "Chassity Madison Waters turned herself into authorities late yesterday afternoon. She has been charged in connection to the homicides of Naja James and Monique Blake. It is still unclear of Ms. Waters' role in the murders. We will continue following this case. More at noon."

David flicked the television off. "Did you see how scared she was?" he asked Brenda, referring to Chassity's mug shot.

Brenda nodded. The fact that Chassity was arrested was almost too much for her to bear, but she knew that she had to hold it together for David.

"Have you spoken with DJ? You should call him before he sees his sister on the news."

David had already spoken to their son DJ the day before. He wanted his son to hear about Monique's death from him. It was important to David to let his son know that Monique was no longer in the picture. He also explained the circumstances along with the information he had at the time concerning her death. DJ had been saddened by all the news. He expressed his sorrows for Ashton and Alex and of course his sister Chassity. He had told his father that he would lay low for a while; he didn't want to be in the mix. Truth was, DJ had already heard. He was visiting his friend out of town.

"Yea, I'll call him later," David responded.

Brenda had searched her heart all morning. She contemplated her words a million times. She still couldn't believe her words, but she said them. "You should also call... um, I think you ... should pay your respects to their family. Naja defended you for years and Monique was important to you."

She exhaled through her nose as she clinched her fist behind her back. David stopped eating, but he didn't look up from his plate. He thought against saying any wrong words. He continued to eat again. Brenda left the bedroom to take a bath. She sat in the bathtub, the steam rose into the air.

DeBAITed Deaths Unknown Face

She smiled as she washed her body. She was able to look at all the things that had brought her to this day. Although the turning point had arrived for their family, she was sad for Chassity, Monique's family, and even Naja. Although her faith was restored, she wanted to shed more tears but she couldn't. Things looked bad but she knew that God was on their side. "Thank You Lord," she said out loud as she looked up into the atmosphere. She prayed more these days, more than any other time in her entire life. Her storm was just beginning when she only saw herself and she now realized that God's spirit stepped in right on time. She was just grateful that she had listened. She prayed.

"Lord, Monique's sons need you more than ever. I ask that you deliver them the peace and understanding that they need as children to know that they are still blessed. I ask that you open their paths to opportunities that will bless them to live life more abundantly. Let them know that their mother may be gone and their father too, but allow them to see, feel, and know that you will be their parents. Have them to recognize that you will provide special blessings in their life. Oh God I ask that they bounce back and grow to be successful men. They shall lead full lives. Bless them Lord, right now in the mighty matchless name of Jesus. Amen."

DeBAITed Deaths Unknown Face

When she opened her eyes, tears flowed freely. Her heart was free; she knew that it was already done. After her long bath, she gave David a bath. She sang his favorite melody by Sam Cooke, *"It's Been a Long Time Coming."* He loved her voice and he loved her again. They played together as they giggled; striving to enjoy their morning in spite of the news. David had explained to Brenda that Anthony cut off her expenses because he couldn't tell which court she was dribbling in. He also explained that the divorce papers had been orchestrated as part of the scheme. He admitted that his plans were to leave but he never knew they were sending her the divorce papers.

"Why were you there that day?" Brenda asked, referring to the information the nurse had given her saying that her husband found her just in time.

"Oh that," he thought. "I wanted to see the place one last time. I never expected to walk in and find you, but I'm glad that I did in time."

After a brief silence, Brenda changed the subject. "Baby, we have a property on the Eastside. It's on the market, but I think we should use it for something."

David was open for the discussion. "What do you have in mind?"

"I was thinking it would make a nice church."

David laughed, "Yea, a church huh?"

Brenda was excited to see him so relaxed. "I am suggesting that we open a church as the owners. Maybe we can help an upcoming pastor or evangelist, you know, give back to the community."

David kissed her forehead. "That's not a bad idea but let's take care of home first."

Brenda let the mood settle by leaving it at that. She stopped drying his body with the towel; she decided to use her tongue instead.

DeBAITed Deaths Unknown Face

She started with his lips, then she kissed his chest and down the length of his tall masculine body. She nibbled his thighs before she kneeled. She tongued his flesh, warming his loins, teasing the head of his full round rod. She opened her mouth. She allowed her tongue to absorb every inch of his anatomy. She tilted her head just enough to take it all in. He watched her as he held her gently by her hair, pulling from the crown of her head. He bit his lip and leaned back into the wall as she bobbed forward continuously. The corner of her lips flowed with his juices while she continued to massage his anatomy and drive him wild. After the long, deep slurps back and forth, he picked her up and propped her against the bathroom counter. His flesh stretched tighter, he penetrated her deep, warm juice box and she exploded as her husband pressed his solid body into hers. They moaned, she begged for more. He went deeper as she held onto his back. During their rhythm, she gazed into his eyes. "Give it to me," she cried.

"Mmmmm," he moaned as he did it harder and faster, over and over again.

She pleasured her husband; he pleased his wife.

DeBAITed Deaths Unknown Face

MONIQUE

Ashton and Alex had just finished eating their cinnamon oatmeal. They sat at the table with their Grandma Lily, Grandpa Freddie, and Uncle Monte. Ashton was getting up to go watch cartoons while Alex was guzzling down his orange juice, in a rush to join his brother.

"We need to talk to you two," Lily said.

The boys came back to the table. They took their seats beside each other. Ashton, Rick's son with Monique, looked up at his grandma with his greenish brown eyes and curly hair. Alex, Mo's son with the late Mike, was African American, his hair cut short, he had big shiny brown eyes. They both were captivated by the sweet, troubled voice of their grandma.

"Your mommy and auntie had an accident," she started slowly. "They were hurt."

Monte sat beside her with his arms folded. He tapped his feet silently under the table. Freddie rubbed over his face; he tried to fight his tears. The boys never knew what had happened to Naja. They always saw her on Sunday, but the last few weeks seemed to have been busy for their family. Mo never got around to telling them.

Ashton asked in his soft, innocent voice, "Where's my daddy grandma?"

Monte intervened, "Hang on man, let grandma finish, okay?"

Ashton nodded. Alex had lost his father in an 'accident' with Rick a few years prior. Sadly he had been through this type of news before. He began to cry.

"Are they dead?" Alex asked.

Everybody fell silent. Their grandma calmly spoke. "Shhh baby, everything is going to be alright. Yes baby, they are gone away."

DeBAITed Deaths Unknown Face

Alex immediately began screaming uncontrollably. Freddie picked him up and took him into the living room. He tried to calm him down. Ashton didn't understand. He sat quietly before he asked, "Are they coming back?"

Their grandma took Ashton by his hand. Lord knows it was hard for her to tell him. Her voice cracked. "No baby, she is gone to be with Jesus."

Ashton still didn't quite understand. He wanted to talk about it. "Who went to live with Jesus grandma, Auntie or my mommy?"

"They both died baby."

Ashton began screaming and stomping his feet. "What about my daddy?" he screamed.

Monte got up. He left the room to help his father console Alex.

"Your daddy is fine baby but you can't see him for a while," she explained.

He was beginning to understand that he couldn't see his mother or his father. His voice turned sad. He was on the verge of tears. "Why grandma? I want my daddy and my mommy. Why can't my daddy come?"

His grandma paused and ran her hands through his hair. Her hands surrounded the cheeks of his soft round face. "Baby, your daddy has to tell the police what happened to your mommy. He has to help them understand her accident. We just have to wait a long time to see him, that's all baby."

Ashton jumped into his grandma's lap. He sobbed. His small arms wrapped tightly around his grandma. She rocked him as she held him close.

Alex wasn't handling the news as well as Ashton. A part of him knew that Rick murdered his mother. Parts of him would *always* remember the arguments they had before his brother was born. The natural part of his bond with his biological father would always tell him that Rick was responsible for his real daddy dying too.

DeBAITed Deaths Unknown Face

"Monte?" Lily called.

Monte hurried into the kitchen. "Ma'am?" he answered.

"Open the kitchen drawer over on the right side of the stove and bring me the Tylenol."

Monte did as he was asked.

"Give them both a little bit before they get too upset. It will help them rest for a little while too."

Monte gave the boys their recommended dosages as his stepmother told him to do. After an hour of rocking the boys, drying their tears, and praying over them, the boys were fast asleep.

By ten that morning Lily was busy cooking, cleaning and preparing for the busy day she expected. Freddie watched Monte mow the yard. He helped him wash the cars. The boys slept peacefully in their grandparent's bed. By noon, the phone began to ring off the hook again. Monte answered most of the calls. Freddie made it clear that they didn't want to speak to anyone. The three of them sat down for lunch shortly after noon. Lily made turkey sandwiches for them with glasses of lemonade. After lunch, Lily began to clean up the table. Monte told his parents that he needed to share a few things with them. Lily sat at the table next to Freddie, across from Monte.

"What is it son?" Freddie asked.

"They have Chassity Waters in custody in connection with both homicides," he stated.

Lily held her focus on Monte. She heard his words. She never spoke too much, she always listened. "Chassity?"

Freddie recalled meeting her at Mo's the night Naja was found.

"I thought she was Mo's friend," Lilly said.

Freddie reasoned as he looked over at his wife. "You were the one who said that she was Monique's friend," he reminded her.

DeBAITed Deaths Unknown Face

Lily snapped back at him. "Hush up Freddie and listen to what Monte is saying to us."

Monte continued, "It's complicated right now. They have a witness, Chassity's boyfriend, who is willing to testify against her with his evidence."

He left out the fact that the witness was his stepbrother. He had to prevent any old rifts from stirring between his father and stepmother. Orlando had been conceived during their marriage. Lily knew that Monte and Freddie would try to manipulate her if she let them. She was determined to speak her peace. She spoke with a hint of conviction in her voice. Her question was asked to let them know that she knew. "Is Brenda off the hook?"

Freddie moved his eyes to Monte as he gradually eased back in his chair. *'Busted'* he thought.

Monte appreciated the silence as he continued. "Well it turns out that Chassity may have done these things in Brenda's defense."

It took all the good in Lily to remain calm. She drove straight to the heart of the point. "Why would she do that to that poor child?"

Monte scrambled to answer. "The authorities no longer believe that Brenda's affiliations are intentional. Chassity is her stepdaughter." There, he finally spat it out.

Freddie froze. "Her what?" he blurted.

All the unknown pieces connected in his head. He wanted to say much more, but he also knew that he should be quiet before he disclosed or confirmed his latest affair.

Lily sat quietly as she scanned their faces. She had an unknown secret as well. They didn't know that Bradley had called to pay his respects. Not only was he Naja's colleague, he had also been acquainted with Monique. Their dishonesty humored Lily. She was disgusted by their unknown confessions. "Well, well, well, let the pieces fall where they may."

DeBAITed Deaths Unknown Face

She stood and left the room and peeped in on the boys.

Monte wanted to talk to Freddie more about the situation but Freddie cut him off. "Not now son, not here. Save this till later!" Freddie demanded.

He left Monte alone while he went to shower and change clothes. Monte stepped out onto the porch with his cell phone and the cordless phone. He sat on the steps while he thought of his sister. He remembered the day they got their tattoos.
He recalled her voice. She always showed her brother her love for him. He and Naja didn't really have a relationship. He never connected with her. She seemed to act like she was better than everyone else. He just didn't care for her. When Monte held his head up, he saw a few people beginning to pull in. One car was his auntie, uncle, and his grandmother. In the other car were a few cousins with their kids. Monte spoke to his loved ones. They hugged and he welcomed everyone in the home. Lily came out onto the porch. She smiled as she welcomed her guests as if it were an ordinary Sunday. By 4 o'clock that afternoon the house was full of relatives, friends, and coworkers of Monique. Some were sad others were still shocked. Most of them held their composure and a few cried. Others spoke softly as they gossiped comparing stories they'd heard.

Ashton and Alex played happily with all the other children; their pain was eased by the peace of the Lord. Monte left for a while. He went home to change clothes and he needed to make a few phone calls. As he drove, he checked his voicemail from his cell phone. Anthony had called him directly. He didn't recognize the phone number so he dialed the number back.

"Yea," Anthony answered.

Monte recognized the voice but he needed to be certain.

"Yea, this is Monte. Wassup?"

"Monte, its Anthony. We need to talk. Can we meet somewhere?"

DeBAITed Deaths Unknown Face

"About what?"

"We need to discuss the direction of things. What's good for you?"

"Now. Meet me at the park behind Frozen Palace in fifteen minutes."

"Cool." Anthony replied.

Monte ended the call. They met alone. Anthony's purpose was to fill any loop holes that would jeopardize Chassity's freedom. Monte backed his Crown Victoria in at the bottom of the park. Anthony pulled his White F-250 in beside Anthony. The two of them were positioned to speak face to face. They nodded at each other. Anthony turned off his engine.

"Wassup?" Monte quizzed.

Anthony began, "What do they have on Chassity that will stick?"

Monte rehearsed his own words in his mind and then he spoke. "My loyalty is with my sister and our family. I can't tell you that."

"I understand that but what I don't understand is how no one can see that Chassity was just in the wrong place at the wrong time. She doesn't have any motive. You got Rick on tape doing Mo himself and we all know Chassity didn't put 3 bullets in Naja's temple at point blank range. Damn it Monte! Where are y'all trying to go with this?" Anthony reasoned.

Monte became agitated. He didn't appreciate Anthony's tone.

"Chassity knows more than what she is telling. Right now it's her word against O's."

Anthony started his engine. The truck jerked after he shifted the gear. He knew they were done talking so he made his final remark.

"Well, it's time Rick starts clearing up some things. But we all know that ain't gonna happen."

DeBAITed Deaths Unknown Face

Anthony was at odds about the entire ordeal. Rick and Monte had been stand up guys in their operation. A part of him hated that Monte lost his sister.

"Aye man, everything that has happened is fucked up and nobody can do anything to fix it. Chassity has been just as loyal to you as she has been to our family. Let's end this," he pleaded.

"If only it was that easy," Monte replied, as he looked Anthony in his eyes. "You said it yourself, I'm in too deep." Anthony left the park. Monte left too. As he drove, he called the D.A.'s office to request that Orlando be put in protective custody. Orlando was only out for himself. He never really cared about Chassity because he knew that his run-ins with her father would never allow them to be together. He could never really trust Chassity. She was too beautiful, too fun and always on the scene. He couldn't handle her care free spirit. She kept him connected, but he didn't need her anymore. He kept Chassity at his mercy for as long as he needed to. He took advantage of the fact that his brother was a detective. In addition, he learned how to get what he wanted through everyone around him, including Anthony. He ran keys of cocaine for Anthony in the past, but business was cut short after Orlando took a plea deal. That's when he gave a statement against David to reduce his sentence. David cut ties with Orlando because of the deception, but that wasn't Anthony's style. Anthony didn't believe in burning bridges with potential connections under any circumstances, plus he knew it was safer to keep Orlando within arm's reach. They were business associates. At the end of the day Orlando was an enemy, and Anthony kept his eyes on all of his enemies.

DeBAITed Deaths Unknown Face

Monte thought about Chassity's role as he drove home. She's the only person who is connected to every single person involved, but he knew that she didn't have a motive. The man is her father and the money is in their family. "D" had already been playing Brenda for years so why would Chassity do it for her? She had never done anything for anybody. Monte wondered if she was playing Mo or keeping tabs on her. He was beginning to have doubts. He spoke to himself, as he pulled in to park his car. "Talk to me Mo. Tell me what happened sis. It's me and you. M&M forever."

DeBAITed Deaths Unknown Face

JASMINE

By the middle of the week Shelton had spoken to David every day since he had been home. The following weekend the two would get to meet for the first time that Shelton could remember. Jasmine had sworn Shelton to secrecy. She wasn't sure how her parents would feel about David stepping in so soon or sudden. Her mother was the secretary of their church. She knocked on her mother's office door.

"Come in," her mother called in her very strong, sweet voice.

"Hey mama," Jasmine spoke as she peeped in to make sure her mother was alone.

"Hey Jas, come on in."

"I was just stopping by to holler at you before I go pick Shelton up from school."

Her mother smiled. She could always tell when Jasmine was up to something. She knew Jas better than she knew herself. Her mother stopped filing the invoices in the drawer. She took her seat behind her desk. "Do tell beauty," her mother smiled.

Jasmine smiled back. Her mother didn't believe in beating around the bush. "David is home mama and he has been calling Shelton every day. He wants to see him next weekend."

Her mother didn't change her mood or her chipper informative tone. "Your father and I already decided what we think would be best for Shelton."

"Which is?"

"We realize that Shelton needs a lot of things including his father. It wasn't until he sent Shelton that letter a few weeks ago that we understood his love for that child. We want what is best for Shelton, not us."

"Am I missing something mama? Are you saying it's okay?"

DeBAITed Deaths Unknown Face

"I am saying that it is okay UNLESS his father shows us in any way that his letters were just a bunch of jail talk!"

Jasmine beamed. "Thank you mama. I can't wait to tell Shelton it's all good!"

Her mother smiled back. "But… her mood changed. She became serious so did her tone. What is going on with Chassity Jas?"

"I don't know mama. I haven't asked "D" any questions."

"Well, you do know she is in jail don't you?"

"Yes ma'am, I know, but Chassity didn't do those things mama."

"I don't want to lose you Jasmine. Now I know you had fallen for that boy Rick. He didn't hurt you or anything did he?"

"Mama, all of that stuff is in the past. Nobody is going to do anything to me. I'm just glad I decided to stay home when I did."

"Why? Are you running from any kind of trouble?"

"No, but I am saying, it could have been me. Chassity and I are tight. We're just on two different levels. I just felt like being home with my family. All of that stuff with Rick happened after I got back. I had just seen Monique, his baby's mama, before I came home. Mama, the world is on a whole other level these days. Anything can happen to anybody, at any time."

"The devil is busy baby. That is why we have to stay prayed up and constantly pray for people in our lives."

"Well, I gotta get ready to go. We are leaving next Friday."

"Who is leaving?"

"Me and Shelton. We are going to spend the weekend in Atlanta."

"You didn't say anything about taking Shelton to Atlanta for the weekend. Jas, you just got finished talking about how you were glad to be home."

DeBAITed Deaths Unknown Face

"We are not going there to live mama. And don't worry about me driving with Shelton by myself. DJ, Chassity's brother, is coming to get us. We are going to try and see Chassity while Shelton spends time with "D." So you ain't got to worry about nothing happening cause "D" is on house arrest during the weekend. He can't leave unless he's going to church mama."

"Church huh? Well, maybe he needs to tell somebody he is going to church and come down here," her mother joked.

"Mama please, c'mon," Jasmine begged.

"It's fine with me, but I have to see what your daddy thinks."

Jasmine knew that if her mother was cool, that her daddy was cool too. "Thank you Mama. I appreciate your blessings. I'm grateful we had this discussion in the house of the Lord," she teased and laughed.

"You knew what you were doing when you came by here." Her mother laughed too. "Is DJ that lil' boy that you've been sneaking to meet all week?" her mother asked.

Whoops. She caught Jas off guard.

"When mama?"

"Girl this town is too small for you to think you fooling anybody."

"He's in town. I saw him and he saw his brother, but we ain't sneaking around," Jasmine giggled.

Her mother giggled too.

"Bye mama, I love you," Jasmine said as she stood to leave.

"I love you more," her mother replied as Jasmine walked out of her office.

Jasmine walked out to her car and called DJ.

"Hey Jas," he answered.

"Hey, I just talked to my mama. Everything is cool."

DeBAITed Deaths Unknown Face

"Good. "D" will be glad to see him and everybody will be glad to see you, especially Brenda. She been stressing lately. I can tell she's just trying to be strong though."

He very seldom referred to Brenda as his mother. He always called her by her name.

"What's going on? What are they saying 'bout Chassity?" Jasmine asked.

His words slurred together. "You don't wanna know."

His tone made Jas sad. "What?" she insisted.

"She's looking at life in prison if convicted."

"LIFE!" Jasmine screamed.

"Yep, I hate you had to hear it from me."

"No, she ain't doing LIFE!"

"I will call you after a while, okay?"

"That's cool. Later," Jasmine ended.

DeBAITed Deaths Unknown Face

DAVID

The couple managed to get their daughter out of jail on a two hundred fifty thousand dollar bond. The judge removed the bond hold after receiving notification that Orlando was ordered to protective custody. Back at the apartment, Brenda had prepared a home cooked meal for her family. They intended to enjoy their dinner and talk to her about her upcoming trial and Orlando. Now outside waiting for her, Chassity ran to the arms of her parents. There were no tears, she was just grateful to be free. She didn't talk to anyone during her stay in the county jail and she had only nibbled the daily meals. Ecstatic to see Brenda, she squeezed her as they held each other tightly. She greeted her daddy with a big kiss and hug as she leaped into his arms.

"I don't know how you made it all of those years in a box. I really appreciate you and all that you have done for me," she told her parents.

They drove back to the apartment. She laid her eyes on a feast of her favorite foods, lasagna, chicken parmesan, Caesar salad, cheesy garlic bread, and a bottle of Merlot.

"Awe thank you, thank you, thank you!" she cheered.

"Go get cleaned up. We will get things in order in here," David instructed.

After a long hot, relaxing bath, Chassity threw on her pink Polo sweat suit and her all white Adidas. "D" and Brenda were sitting at the table waiting. When Chassity arrived, they blessed the food.

After a few bites of his dinner, "D" asked, "Have you called your mother?"

Chassity twisted on the inside. Her mother had never really been there for her. She always seemed to judge her instead of support her.

DeBAITed Deaths Unknown Face

"I called but before I could say anything she told me to stay wherever I have been staying at, that this is my mess and that she would pray for me. So I hung up and didn't bother to call back."

David looked across at his wife. They shared eye contact as they continued eating dinner. David took the time to choose his words carefully.

"Chassity, I am not upset with you for dating "O". You were younger when things happened between him and me. It was business and we both made bad decisions, but I just can't help feeling like he used you to get back at me and to cut his parole time. He turned state evidence against you baby. Now I have to ask you, what is it that he knows that may hurt you?"

Chassity stopped eating. She sat back in the chair and folded her arms across her chest. She wouldn't look up, her eyes were full of tears. She felt nasty inside. Moments passed before David and Brenda stopped eating as well. Brenda reached across the table. She clenched Chassity's hand.

"Talk to us baby."

"I just want to help you," David assured.

"I don't know what he could have said against me. I never said anything to anyone. I just watched like I was supposed to. I called Monique right before Rick killed Naja."

David knew he was breaking through to her. He could tell that she was hiding something, she didn't look as confident as she did in the beginning. Chassity replayed the events in her mind. He became nervous.

"Why did you call her?"

She spoke her truth this time…all of it. "Rick told me to make sure she was okay after Naja exposed their plot. He became nervous and began thinking that somebody might hurt her or the boys." She stopped talking.

"What is it?" David asked.

DeBAITed Deaths Unknown Face

Chassity surrendered the missing information. "He knew where I was going. He had to have known because he dropped me off when we got back into town. Orlando had called but I didn't have my phone. Rick took it after I talked to Mo and I got a new one when we got back into town."

David's mind was unfolding Rick's movements. He knew how Rick operated. He knew Chassity and he knew Monte but he had to understand "O's" position.

"Who all knew about their plot?" David asked.

"Rick, Monte, Me, and O." The thought of Orlando's betrayal made Chassity sick. Even saying his name disgusted her.

"Did anyone see you with Rick at the scene?" David asked feeling a lump in his throat.

Chassity sighed, "I only saw one car pass us but Rick was wiping down the car and his head was down. I was in costume.

"Gloves?" David inquired.

"No, I didn't know I would need any. I didn't know Rick was going to kill her. He told me to drive and that's it.

"What did you drive that day?'

Chassity looked up at her father. Her eyes flinched the same way they had when she ran to Brenda for help. Her tone was shaky and low.

"A tow truck, but we ditched it. I drove my rental back into town. It wasn't one of your company trucks."

Her words trailed off. Things had happened so fast that she had been completely oblivious to any of it. Suddenly, Chassity became very upset. She slowly recalled the play in her mind, realizing that she had indeed committed a crime.

David didn't waste any time. "What kind of car passed you? THINK Chassity! This is important," He yelled again. "THINK DAMN IT!"

DeBAITed Deaths Unknown Face

Chassity held her forehead trying to focus. Brenda held her heart as she stared at Chassity. Chassity started to speak but then she stopped. It was coming to her now.

"I don't know, I think it was... an uh, uh... she hit her hand against the table. A Caprice!" She finally remembered. She was glad that she remembered.

David didn't ask any more questions. Instead, he stood, grabbed his keys and announced, "I gotta see Anthony," and he left.

Chassity and Brenda continued to sit at the table. Chassity was confused as she looked up at Brenda; Brenda was unsettled on the inside. She knew that Chassity had been placed at the scene. She was willing to bet her life savings that it was the proof against Chassity. She didn't show her feelings or reveal her thoughts,

"You just got home. Let's go cuddle, watch Lifetime together to take our minds off things for a little while," Brenda suggested.

Chassity agreed silently, she nodded. The two took the rest of the wine into the bedroom and turned on the television.

Meanwhile, David rushed to his house, the one he shared with Brenda. It was the only safe place that he could think of.

Anthony was already in the driveway when David arrived. "What's going on?" Anthony asked "D" as he got out of his truck.

"Not out here," D stated as he unlocked the door. The two of them covered their noses when they entered the home. All of the food had rotted and the trash was still in the trashcans. "Get a crew over here to clean the house," he called out as he opened a few windows and turned on the ceiling fans. Anthony did as he was told.

"What the hell is going on?" Anthony demanded, getting back to business.

DeBAITed Deaths Unknown Face

David sat at the large oval glass kitchen table. He told Anthony about Chassity's connection to Naja's death. When he mentioned the tow truck and the Chevy Caprice, Anthony shouted, "MONTE!"

"That's what I'm thinking," D revealed. And he had "O" to cover him. Orlando was in it for his cut of the money that Naja thought she was going to get."

"Rick trusted Monte and Monte trusted Orlando."

Anthony became very angry, very fast. "Damn! We gotta tell Frells. DAMN IT "D"! Chassity could go down in this even if Rick does give a statement!"

David shook his head, dismissing the possibility. "Rick ain't gonna talk."

Anthony called attorney Frells who agreed to meet them where they were. Within the hour the cleaning crew was mopping the floors, cleaning the dishes and completing the laundry. Mr. Frells arrived almost 2 hours after Anthony's call. "D" had to report to his parole officer so he didn't have much time to meet.

As soon as Mr. Frells got in the house, David and Anthony brought him up to speed on the information Chassity provided. Mr. Frells was very concerned. He did not like the situation. He also had bad news to share. His voice was very deep and stern. He was genuinely concerned. He propped his forearms against his thighs as he sat at the edge of the couch. His tone was low. "There is more. We have a copy of the wire from Ms. James vehicle. I have also reviewed the tape recording from the murder of Ms. Blake. There was also an audio recording taped from the home of Ms. Blake around the same time Ms. James was murdered."

Chassity was in too deep. Anthony kicked the edge of the couched and put his hands into his pocket. He began pacing.

"What's on the tape?" David asked.

DeBAITed Deaths Unknown Face

"Well, it sounds like Chassity made the call to distract Ms. Blake. It seems that she tried to use Ms. Blake as her alibi. She made several calls to the home regarding borrowing a hundred dollars. The troubling part about the encounter is that she was also at the scene shortly after Ms. Blake received the news that her sister had been found dead."

David and Anthony were speechless. "D's" voice turned raspy. "What can we do?"

Mr. Frells took a deep breath. "Well, I was about to call you into my office. They have offered a plea."

The evidence was there. They knew it. Damn! Anthony was furious. He knew he needed to find Orlando as soon as possible.

David dreaded hearing the answer to the question that he was about to ask. "What is it?"

Mr. Frells looked David straight in the eye. "If she pleads guilty to conspiracy to commit murder and involuntary manslaughter, she will avoid a jury trial. Let me tell you Mr. Carter, I think she should take the deal. We both know that if certain things really unfold, it could get real ugly."

David cleared his throat. Mr. Frells was right. "How much time will she do?" he asked.

Mr. Frells shifted in his seat. Anthony stopped pacing and practically held his breath as he waited for the answer.

"The offer is 25 serve 10."

"NO! She didn't plan to kill anybody. She only knew about Naja's death. C'mon Frells, is that the best you can do?"

Mr. Frells held up his hand. "Mr. Carter, I may be able to get the conspiracy charge dropped to a lesser charge, but she will have to testify against Mr. Shaw in open court. The D.A is asking for the death penalty in this case. Rick would be on death row."

DeBAITed Deaths Unknown Face

Anthony couldn't process the news. He threw up both his hands and walked out the front door letting it slam as he left. David looked at his watch realizing that he had to report to his parole officer within the hour. He sighed, "Give me time to talk to my daughter. Can you do that?"

Mr. Frells stood. "We have the weekend Mr. Carter. We have to act fast. Your daughter has to be in my office by 9:00 am Monday."

David extended his hand to close the deal. As they shook hands, "She will be there," he said.

Frells left. David yelled for the cleaning crew to leave. They walked through the house to make sure nothing was left behind as he inspected their work. The cleaning crew was dismissed. As David paced from room to room, he was lost in his thoughts. I've known Rick since he was a kid. Damn! I should have just told the truth. None of this would have happened. He blinked away his tears. He grew angrier and he blamed himself for destroying so many lives.

He fell to his knees. *"God, I will do whatever I have to do to fix this. Use me and show me how to fix this. Amen."*

DeBAITed Deaths Unknown Face

JASMINE

Their special weekend finally arrived. Shelton was ecstatic to finally meet his father. The last few weeks had been very emotional. Jasmine was grateful that DJ stepped up to the plate to form a bond with Shelton. Although Shelton lost his mother, he would soon gain the presence of his father. DJ called ahead to let his parents know that he, Jasmine, and Shelton were on their way. The ride was quiet and peaceful for the most part. No one really knew what to expect but Jasmine was grateful for the union. She was more excited to see Chassity. They had a lot of things to discuss. DJ glanced at his brother as he drove. His thoughts were of his youth. He reminisced over how his father used to be with him. As an adult, he was beginning to understand how all of those actions rooted the incidents that had occurred. It was important for DJ to rescue his brother. He was determined to put his foot down with his parents. He felt that he needed to let them know that it was time out for their selfish ways. The 90 minute drive wore Shelton out; he had fallen asleep. Jasmine wanted him to be bright eyed a bushy tailed when he met his father, stepmother and sister.

"Let's pull into this gas station so Shelton can put his other shirt on. This one is wrinkled," Jasmine said to DJ as she pulled into the Texaco station on her right.

Shelton was too cute in his Levi denim jeans, his black Eastland shoes and his freshly pressed white button down shirt. His auntie brushed over his soft, reddish hair. She looked into his grey eyes.

"We are five minutes away baby. Are you excited?"

"Yes ma'am. I am ready," Shelton readily replied.

DJ made another call telling his parents they were minutes away. Jasmine felt the excitement in the air. She became a little nervous as they approached the apartment complex. She thought of Rick. It had been a week.

DeBAITed Deaths Unknown Face

Monique would be laid to rest on Sunday. She blinked the images away as DJ parked. She helped Shelton out of the car and they followed DJ to the steps that led up to the apartment. Shelton counted to himself with each step.

He laughed. "We are almost at the top."

"You are on your way honey," Jasmine agreed as she took each step behind him. DJ knocked at the door but no one answered. He knocked again.

"Come in," his mother Brenda called.

DJ opened the door. He allowed Shelton and Jasmine to walk in first.

"WELCOME, WELCOME, WELCOME!" Everyone yelled.

Shelton stood stiff at the front door, smiling. Jasmine became overwhelmed as she looked around the room full of balloons with attached pictures on the end. David kept every picture of Shelton that Tawanna had ever mailed him. They were all hanging from the ceiling tile. David kneeled down in front of his son. Shelton felt his presence. He put his hands all over his father's face then began to wipe his father's tears.

"Don't cry Daddy," he whispered.

David swept his son off the floor and hugged him tightly. Jasmine and Chassity ran to each other, they shared a tearful embrace. DJ wrapped his arms around his mother. He felt that things were different. He now knew that his family had changed. Anthony was also there. He pushed a cart full of presents into the living room for Shelton. The day had been full of emotions for David. The evening arrival of his son's visit made the morning hardships disappear for the moment. David gathered himself together.

"I want to spend time with Shelton alone," he announced.

Brenda reminded David of the time. His parole required him to be home by eleven certain nights. "It's already after seven. Why not get a fresh start in the morning?" she asked.

Anthony knew that "D" wouldn't hear of anything other than what he wanted to do.

DeBAITed Deaths Unknown Face

He interceded. "I will take you two wherever you wanna go. Don't worry "B". I will get them back in time."

David released Shelton long enough for him to hug his auntie. His father picked him up again and they left out of the door. Once they were gone, DJ made everyone aware that he didn't want to be the only man in the room. He invited his mother to dinner. His plan was to take advantage of the opportunity to speak up for his brother's well-being. Brenda was more than grateful to take her son up on his offer. They left out for dinner.

Now Jasmine and Chassity were alone. Jasmine didn't waste any time catching up with her friend.

"What is going on? You look good! How are you holding up?" she rambled.

Chassity smirked at her friend. She shook her head,

"I'm doing. I thought about going to Mo's funeral, but I can't take the chance of seeing "O." Girl, I can't believe how he is trying to set me up."

"How is he doing that? What do you mean?"

Chassity raised her hands up and dropped her head out of disbelief. "The shit is crazy now that I think about it. He is just being real low down, twisting things his way. I don't even wanna talk about that because I know that I am innocent. What is going on with you? I haven't seen you in a dress or leggings since we were like twelve years old. I know you better not be trying to push up on my brother with your fast butt," Chassity teased.

Jasmine looked at her friend in her eyes. Her demeanor became stressed. Jasmine had a secret. Chassity knew it.

"Tell me wassup Jas."

"Girl, I'm pregnant."

"WHAT?"

Jasmine revealed the details. "No one knows but you. I took a pregnancy test at home the other night. It was positive and I'm going to the doctor on Tuesday."

DeBAITed Deaths Unknown Face

"WHAT?" Chassity yelled again.

"It's Rick's," Jasmine said then dropped her head.

"Hell to the NO!" Chassity blurted. "What are you going to do?"

Jasmine held her head up. She looked at Chassity in disbelief of her question.

"I am going to have *this* baby."

Chassity understood.

DeBAITed Deaths Unknown Face

MONIQUE

The atmosphere although somber was also very peaceful. Her mother had arranged a beautiful service. Family, friends, co-workers, neighbors, and even the Carter family attended with Jasmine. Chassity was very emotional as she clenched her father's hand. They all sat in the balcony away from the immediate family. David longed for the intimacy, love, and understanding that he and Monique once shared. The complexity of the situation left Brenda at ease. Her heart ached for a woman who her husband still loved. Ashton and Alex stood with teary eyes. They both left roses for their mother on her casket.

After the repast, the Carter's walked towards Anthony's Navigator prepared to leave. Monte stopped David,

"Aye "D", he called. He sounded as if he *needed* to see him.

David had hoped to dodge Monte, the children and her parents. He only wanted to bid farewell to the lady who once shared his heart. He heard Monte's voice but it was his tone that caused him to stop. He knew Monte wanted him to say something to him.

"Yea Monte?" David turned to face him.

The two stood face to face for a few moments. David broke the silence.

"Monte, I wish that I could change all of this. I feel partly responsible. I loved your sister and I am very sorry for the loss your family has endured."

Monte held his stance with his hands in his pocket. He finally spoke. "You are not the only one to blame in this and it's good to see you home."

The men looked at each other. History transpired between the two of them. They embraced one another and patted each other's back.

"Take care," Monte insisted.

DeBAITed Deaths Unknown Face

"No hard feelings," replied David.

For Monte, his sister's death validated his affair with David's wife.

It was over. The storm had passed. There was nothing anyone could do to change the turmoil that would affect their fate.

*   *   *   *   *   *   *   *   *

The following Thursday they would meet in court. Monique's mother would hear the story unfold. The facts were unbearable and at times she would leave the hearing. Freddie could never make her understand how or why he let things transpire. Brenda never attended the hearings. She and DJ prepared their home for the arrival of Shelton.

The day Monique quit her job, Liz's assistant had taken the call and forwarded the call to Liz who placed Monique on a personal leave of absence and forged her signature on her benefits package. Ashton and Alex would now receive substantial monetary benefits annually. Liz, the culprit of the phone calls had also been drawn in too deep and she felt that her deed had righted all of her wrongs.

Chassity's dreams of graduating from Spellman the following fall semester and her intentions of pursuing her Masters' degree in Education were shattered after the jury found her guilty of two lesser charges, concealing a death and involuntary manslaughter. She was sentenced ten years serve five. Once incarcerated her health screen revealed that she was HIV negative. Her careless sex, with her carefree bisexual boyfriend had not impacted her life.

Orlando was released from protective custody. He left town after the trial. He moved on to another town carelessly sleeping with men and women spreading his unknown virus.

Monte insisted on raising his nephews and he did.

DeBAITed Deaths Unknown Face

Lily divorced Freddie and moved back north. She eventually forgave her ex-husband and his sons. She had the peace of the Lord when she died.

Jasmine visited Rick once when their son was three years old. He still didn't speak of his role nor did he speak of his children. He had only told Jasmine to take care of his child and to someday find a way to unite him with his brothers. Those were Rick's only words before his execution.

Anthony helped Jasmine raise Rick's son. Somehow, they filled the void of the bond they had broken once before.

David and Brenda renewed their wedding vows. The couple started their church and opened several other shelters for battered women and children.

* * * * * * * * *

Years later, Alex became a judge in criminal court. His reputation was that of a judge who gave no breaks and passed out harsh sentences. Ashton became a congressman. He was a very out spoken advocate against domestic violence. Although they grew up to be successful and accomplished men, the events of their childhood still plagued them. Not a day passed by when the two brothers didn't think of their mother or the people who played a part in her death. As they met for lunch in the lobby of the Twelve Hotel in downtown Atlanta, they both knew this meeting was about more than just lunch.

"What's going on man?" Alex greeted Ashton as he put his arms around his shoulders.

"We have our orders," Ashton replied.

"Yeah, I spoke with Bradley about that. He's ready to coach the final game."

Their positions of power would make revenge that much sweeter.

To be continued....

DeBAITed Deaths Unknown Face

About the Author:

"Hi readers, I am ecstatic about the possibilities of "DeBAITed Deaths Unknown Face –Part II".

Please feel free to contact me at: LynJackson.nvr@gmail.com

Thanks for your support.

Sincerely,
Author Kolendra J.

www.ingramcontent.com/pod-product-compliance
Lightning Source LLC
Chambersburg PA
CBHW071216090426
42736CB00014B/2845